W9-CXJ-875

# THE PATHS OF PREHISTORY IN PERIGORD

TEXT
JEAN-LUC AUBARBIER AND MICHEL BINET

PHOTOGRAPHS
JEAN-PIERRE BOUCHARD

Translation: Entreprises 35

Éditions Ouest-France

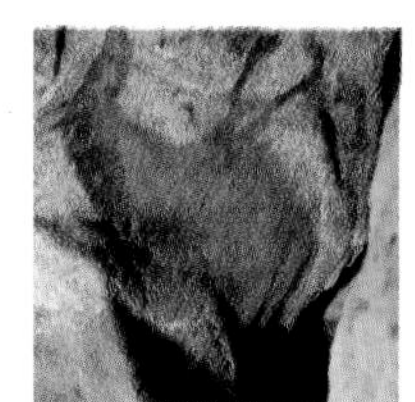

# A word to the visitor

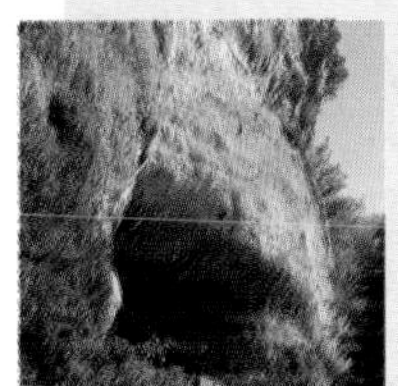

*From the dawn of the first Homo sapiens until our day, via Gallo-Roman Antiquity and the Christian era, Périgord is one of the rare regions on this planet to present the complete history of humanity. For the period 100,000 to 10,000 B.C. it was unquestionably the centre of the prehistoric world, with its thousands of sites and more than half the decorated caves of France... it is an essential heritage of humanity. Recent discoveries (Fronsac, Jovelle, Font-Bargeix) make us think that there are even more marvels waiting to be found. When you visit Périgord, you can never be sure whether or not your footsteps are echoing in some underground cave of inestimable beauty, even finer than the Lascaux cave!*

*The science of Prehistory is a young science. Local farmers, the latest to work these prehistoric grounds, and priests and teachers who asked themselves questions about the origin of Man, were the first of the ranks of prehistorians. Today they have ceded their place to scientists and speleologists, specialists who rely on modern discoveries. The non-accredited visitor must therefore never do any digging himself, nor collect any stones or embark on any dangerous exploration, in order to safeguard this essential heritage of humanity. The Prehistory of Périgord is the personal possession of every human being in search of his origins, beautiful and moving, even for the non-initiated. It is the cultural possession of Man in just the same way as the pyramids of Egypt or the Parthenon of Athens. Prehistory is still too little known, and Périgord should be on everyone's itinerary, a pilgrimage dedicated to the cult of knowledge and beauty, the cult of eternity.*

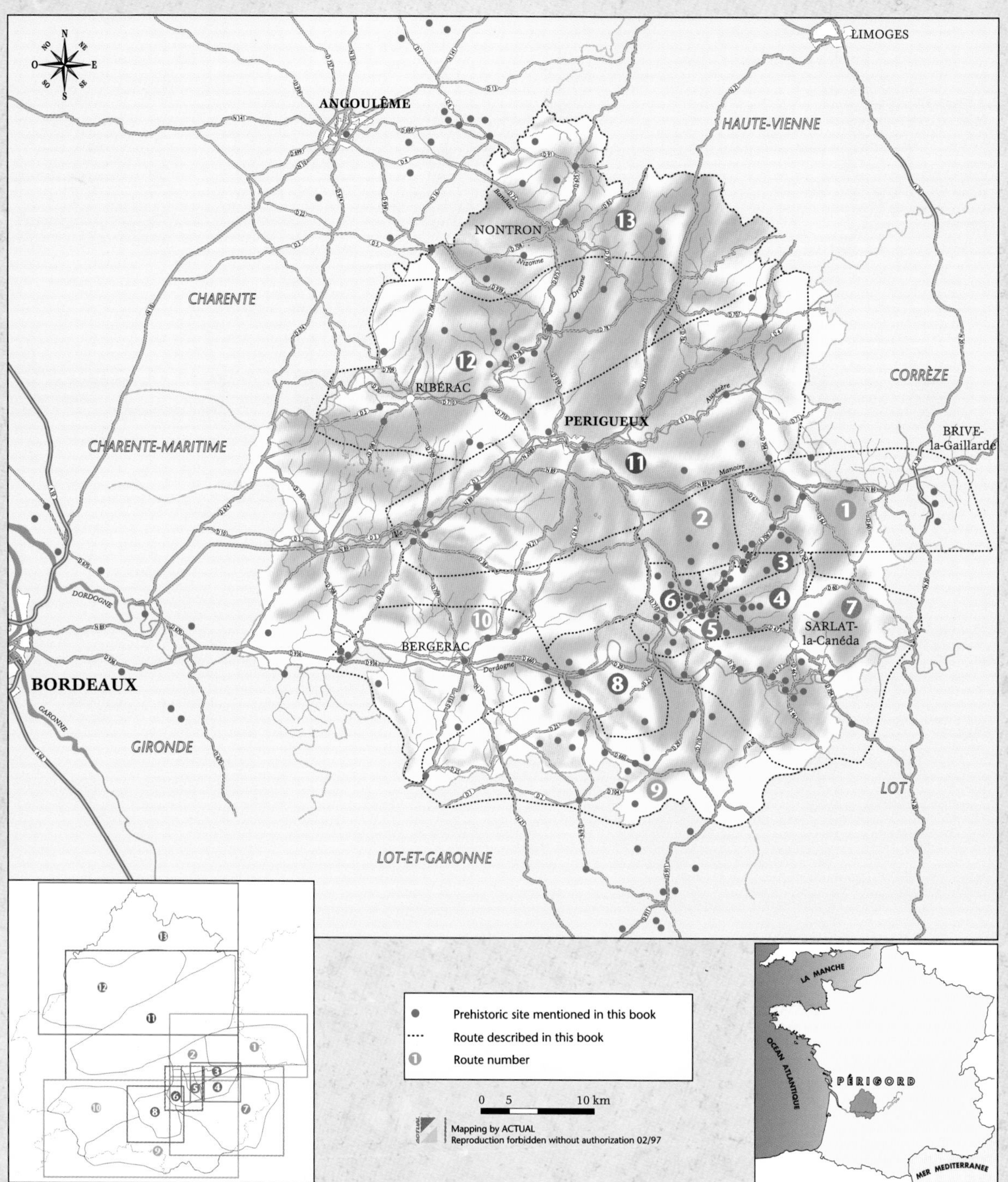


## How to use this guide

- To find information about a specific site:

  ☞ consult the index at the end of the book

- To find sites belonging to a geographical area, to organize a tour, or to follow one of the routes suggested:

  ☞ see the contents at the end of the book or the general map above

  ☞ then study the detailed map, read the practical information and descriptions.

**At Les Eyzies, the cliff hides the Grand Roc cave with its concretions.**

## Prehistoric Périgord

*Can one talk about Prehistoric Périgord? Naturally the Dordogne département, which used to be Périgord county, had no legal existence in prehistoric times! However, if you study the distribution of prehistoric sites on a map, both in France and the whole world, it is easy to spot that, in the years 100,000 to 10,000 B.C., the Périgord region had an extraordinary number of caves, rock shelters and sites of great importance. The idea of Prehistoric Périgord goes beyond the borders of the département, so we shall also consider the Charentais sites between Angoulême and Périgord, those near Brive, in Corrèze, Fumel, in Lot-et-Garonne, Cougnac in the Lot, and the sites on the banks of the river Dordogne, in Gironde, between Castillon-la-Bataille and Bordeaux. If one defines a zone such as this, not going more than 20 kilometres (12 miles) beyond the Dordogne borders, one finds about 100 decorated caves and shelters out of the 173 known in France (23 in the neighbouring Quercy region, 27 for the Pyrenees, and 17 for the Rhône-Mediterranean region).*

| Date | Period | Human types | Tools | Art and religion | | Industries |
|---|---|---|---|---|---|---|
| - 3.5 m. yrs.<br>- 2 m. yrs.<br>- 500 000 yrs. | Lower Palaeolithic | Australanthropian<br>Australopithecus<br>Zinjanthropian | Worked pebbles | | | Abbevillian, Acheulian |
| - 250 000 | | Archanthropian<br>Pithecanthropian<br>Sinanthropian<br>Atlanthropian | controlled fires<br>bifaces<br>huts | cannibalism (?) | | |
| - 100 000<br>- 50 000 | Middle Palaeolithic | Paleanthropian<br>Neanderthal<br>Fontéchevade<br>Swanscombe | points<br>scrapers<br>bifaces | use of ochres<br>collection of shells | | Micoquian, Mousterian |
| - 35 000<br>- 30 000 | Upper Palaeolithic | Néanthropian (Homo Sapiens Sapiens):<br>Combe-Capelle<br>Cro-Magnon | double faced knives | Bone and shell jewellery engraved female representations | sepulchres dug in pits, decorated with objects | Châtelperronian, Perigordian, Aurignacian |
| - 25 000 | | | scrapers<br>spears | female statuettes<br>animal engravings | | Gravettian |
| - 20 000 | | Grimaldi | burins | development of painting | | Solutrean |
| - 15 000 | | | laurel-leaf points, needles with eyes | | | Magdalenian |
| - 12 000 | | Chancelade | spear-throwers<br>harpoons | Important work on decorated caves, portable art | | |
| - 9000 | Epipalaeolithic | | deer antler engravings | end of cave wall art | | Azilian |
| - 8000<br>- 7000 | Mesolithic | | Microliths<br>bows, arrow points | | | Sauveterrian |
| - 5000<br>- 3000 | Neolithic | | Polished stones<br>Agriculture, cattle breeding land-clearing, pottery | | Dolmens and Megaliths * | Artenacian |
| - 2000 | Copper Age (Chalcolitic) | | Copper tools | | | |
| - 800 | Bronze Age | | Bronze tools (tin and copper alloy) | Gold and bronze jewellery | | |
| - 50 | Iron Age | | Iron tools | | Funeral urns | |

* Collective sepulchral caves, trepanning.

***The river Vézère near the huge La Madeleine shelter, at Tursac.***

## La Vézère, "the Valley of Man"

*The river Vézère has its source on the Millevaches plateau, to begin its course of 192 kilometres (120 miles). In Limousin, it waters Treignac and Uzerche, skirts Brive where the Corrèze joins it, and then enters Périgord at Terrasson. After Montignac, where Lascaux looks down on it from high above, it starts its "royal journey through Prehistory". Right until it joins the Dordogne at Limeuil, the sheer beauty of the sites - abrupt cliffs overhanging the river, rock shelters, troglodyte strongholds, castles reflected in the water - competes with the extraordinary archeological interest of this unique concentration of prehistoric sites (decorated rock shelters and caves), most dating back to the middle or early Palaeolithic era (100,000 to 10,000 B.C.). This prehistoric circuit, "the Valley of Man", which is incontestably the most important and the most beautiful on our planet, has been classified as a "world heritage" by UNESCO. And such a precaution is not exaggerated. Let us judge for ourselves. After Lascaux, the magic cave, the river Vézère glides past the châteaux of Losse and Belcayre, passes close by the Knights Templar village of Sergeac and the prehistoric and troglodyte sites of Castelmerle, waters Saint-Léon and its fine church, separates the site of Moustier, eponym of Mousterian and the huge troglodyte fortress of La Roque-Saint-Christophe, and then reflects the Madeleine cliff, which gave its name to the Magdalenian era where Prehistory and the early and late Middle Ages meet. You think you must have seen everything... but the visit is only just beginning. Next comes Les Eyzies, the world capital of Prehistory. The infinity of its prehistoric sites, the quality of its decorated caves (Font-de Gaume, les Combarelles, La Mouthe and its National Museum of Prehistory housed in a castle, have no rival apart from the exceptional beauty of the site with its huge cliffs and carved out rock shelters. Downstream from Les Eyzies, the surroundings become even more splendid as if nature and time together wanted to reduce man himself to the dimensions of an epiphenomenon. The route taken by the Vézère runs under cliffs with prestigious rock shelters - Laugerie, Haute and Basse, the Gorge d'Enfer - and pierced by both natural caves (Grand-Roc, Carpe-Diem) and artificial caves (Roc de Tayac). What other valley can rival the Vézère here, apart from the Nile and the Valley of Kings! After Les Eyzies, there are still other discoveries to be made in its company: the castle of Campagne, Le Bugue with its decorated caves of Saint-Cirq and Bara-Bahau, and its Proumeyssac chasm. And then, finally, the Vézère mingles calmly with the waters of the Dordogne at the foot of the high-perched village of Limeuil.*

***Gorge d'Enfer, Les Eyzies.***

# Introduction

This book is not intended to be a treatise on Prehistory. It is not addressed to professional prehistorians but, in a much more modest way, to the visitor interested in Prehistory who wishes to discover the extent of the wealth of Dordogne.

Thanks to Boucher de Perthes and above all to Darwin, we now know that there was no spontaneous creation. Man did not appear *ex nihilo* out of a magician's hat six thousand years ago, as had long been believed. He developed from a lower form of life and his present morphology and psychism are the result of a very long evolutionary process. And, in addition to this, the rate of evolution was not the same at each instant everywhere on the planet. Neanderthal man did not wake up one bright morning to find he had changed into Cro-Magnon man. Thus one cannot talk about continuous linear evolution and no evolutive scheme can be entirely exact.

***The Lartet shelter in the Gorge d'Enfer (Les Eyzies).***

***Opposite page: The river Vézère, "Valley of Man": the panorama from the Jor hill, near Moustier.***

But, even so, the science of prehistory and all its associated and complementary disciplines have enabled us to draw up a fairly accurate picture of our ancestors; their morphology, their way of life and their surroundings. This certainly gives a fairly accurate idea but it is not definitive, since if we do not possess irrefutable data, accounts of Prehistory will still remain in the conditional tense. Prehistorians have to interpret the traces of a past which is irremediably gone for ever and must be prudent in their hypotheses. What do we really know at present about our past?

One of our most distant ancestors, called Ramapithecus, lived in Africa 14 million years ago. He was a small monkey. Two parallel branches came after him: one leading to the big monkeys of nowadays, and the other to Man. Between 7 and 1 million years ago Australopithecus lived in Africa. He used flat stones and stone chippings. Was he a man, or a pre-man as is generally thought? We shall leave this to the specialists to decide, and ask ourselves the essential question. When can one really begin to talk about Man? The first being who merits this description is Homo habilis. He lived about 2 million years ago, mainly in Africa. A contemporary of Australopithecus, described as robust, this capable man without doubt possessed clear hominoid tendencies. He was small in height, (1.5 metres or 5 ft), his cranial capacity was 500 cubic centimetres (30 cu. in.), and he walked upright. He used tools (shaped stones) which enabled him to hunt, but above all he passed on his experience to his descendants. Did he speak an articulate language? One can neither confirm nor deny this. Nonetheless, he represents an essential stage between Australopithecus and the Archanthropians or Homo erectus.

These «upright men» lived almost alone on the planet between 1.5 million years and 200,000 years ago. There are

traces of *Homo erectus* in many places: in Java, the Maghreb, in China and in Eastern Africa. He was two-footed, about 1.5 metres tall (5 ft), and his cranial volume could be greater than 1,000 cubic centimetres (60 cu. in.). Above his eye-sockets there were bony brow-ridges. He lived next to rivers, in caves or huts. He was very specialized. His industry was of the Acheulian type (biface, scraper). He hunted and made fires.

The first traces of hearths date back to 600,000 B.C. The Archanthropians are our ancestors. But where, when and how did this transition to modern man take place? We are not very certain. On the other hand, in Europe, around 700,000 B.C.

one can already see signs of changes leading little by little to the Paleanthropians, among them Neanderthal man. He was present everywhere in the Ancient World between 100,000 and 35,000 B.C. He was short (1.55 metres or 5 ft. 1 in.) and heavy. His cranial volume was already equal to or greater than our own. He had a receding forehead, still with bony brow-ridges above the eye sockets, but today we know that his real morphology was half-way between the animal-type representation of the statue at Les Eyzies and our own. He possessed a wide range of tools of Mousterian type: points, cutters, scrapers, bifaces, borers etc. He did not use bone very much, but probably worked with wood.

Neanderthal man probably disappeared around 35,000 B.C. It now seems clear that he was only one of the cousins of the Neanthropians (*Homo sapiens sapiens*) whose most famous representatives are Cro-Magnon man, Combe-Capelle, Grimaldi and Chancelade men. This Cro-Magnon type man, who appeared about 35,000 years ago, worked mainly with reindeer antlers, bone and ivory. His lithic industry was extremely fine. The development of his psychism and social needs led him to create art. He engraved, painted and sculpted. At the dawn of History, his direct descendants became farmers and, in 1969, walked on the Moon.

*Tayac rock (Les Eyzies).*

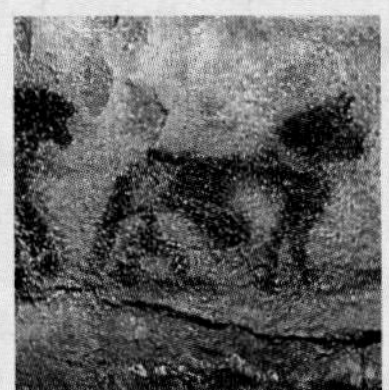

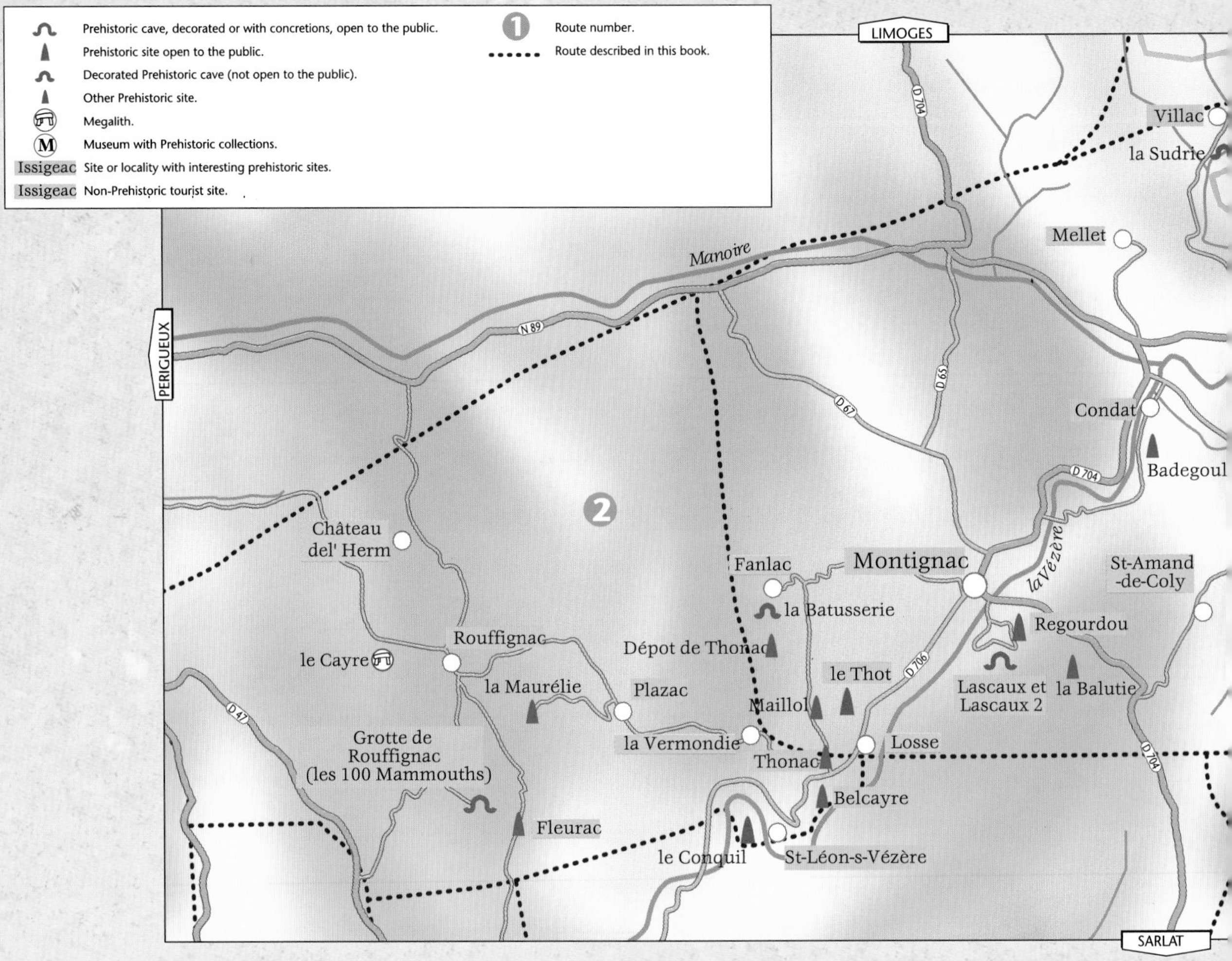

Prehistoric cave, decorated or with concretions, open to the public.
Prehistoric site open to the public.
Decorated Prehistoric cave (not open to the public).
Other Prehistoric site.
Megalith.
Museum with Prehistoric collections.
Issigeac Site or locality with interesting prehistoric sites.
Issigeac Non-Prehistoric tourist site.
Route number.
Route described in this book.

LIMOGES
PERIGUEUX
SARLAT
D 704
Villac
la Sudrie
Mellet
Manoire
N 89
D 65
D 67
Condat
Badegoul
D 704
Château del' Herm
Fanlac
Montignac
la Vézère
St-Amand -de-Coly
la Batusserie
Regourdou
le Cayre
Rouffignac
Dépot de Thonac
le Thot
D 706
Lascaux et Lascaux 2
la Balutie
la Maurélie
Plazac
Maillol
D 47
Grotte de Rouffignac (les 100 Mammouths)
la Vermondie
Losse
Thonac
D 704
Belcayre
Fleurac
le Conquil
St-Léon-s-Vézère

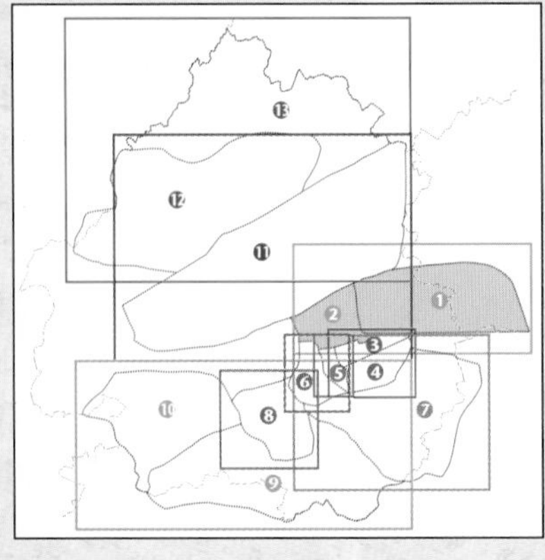



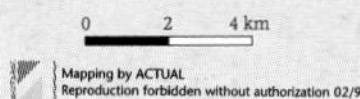

# Lascaux, Rouffignac, Saint-Léon-sur-Vézère

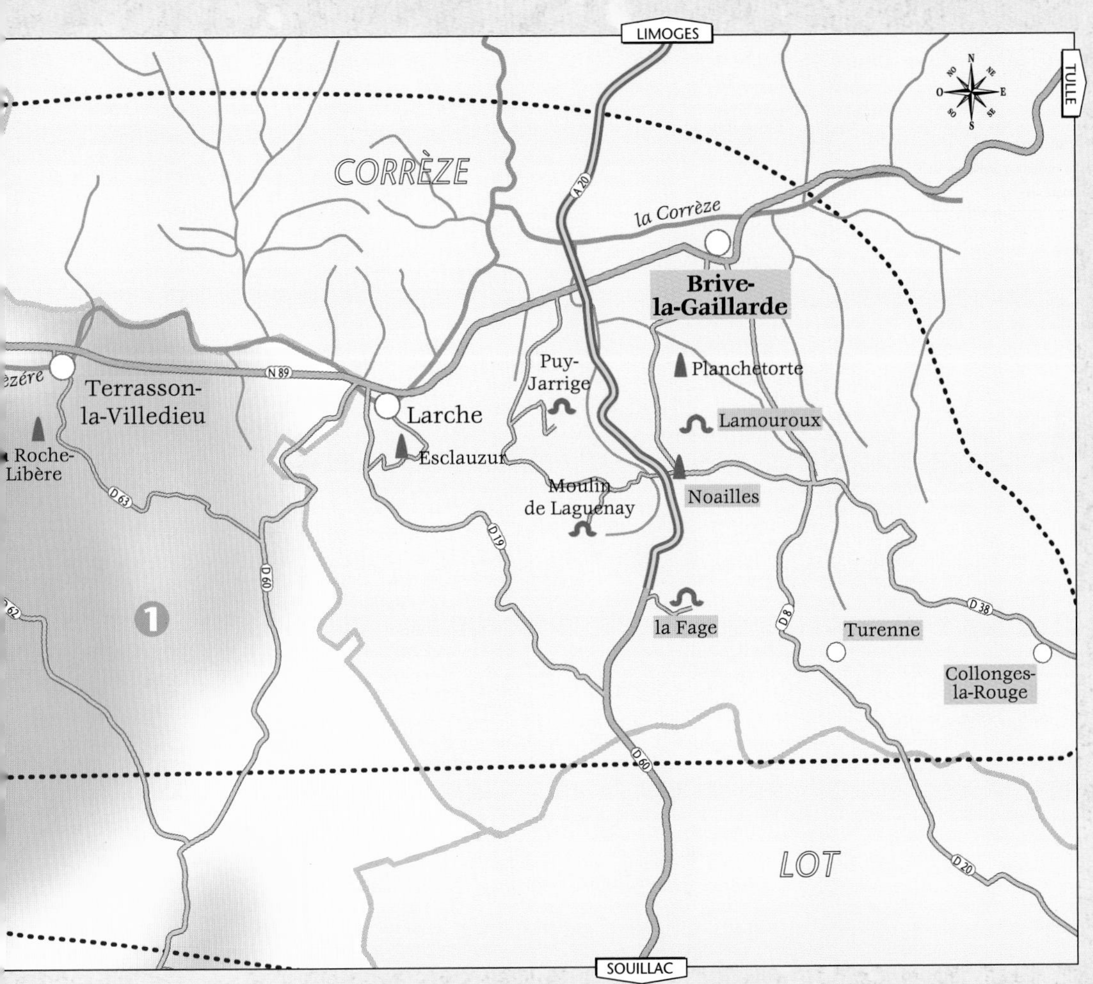


## Sites open to visitors around Montignac-Lascaux

**Lascaux II** facsimile, tel. 05.53.51.82.60.
**Régourdou** prehistoric site, tel. 05.53.51.81.23.
**Thot** centre of prehistoric art, tel. 05.53.50.70.44.
**La Fage** chasm, tel. 05.55.85.80.35. or 05.55.85.81.14.
**Lamouroux** caves
**Montignac** Tourist Bureau, tel. 05.53.51.83.60.
**Terrasson** Tourist Office, tel. 05.53.50.37.56.
**Brive** Tourist Office, tel. 05.55.24.08.80.

*Walkers can follow the GR 36 from Saint-Léon-sur-Vézère to Montignac, via the Vermondie and the Thot, and then the GR 461 as far as Lascaux. Do not miss the Saint-Amand-de-Coly abbey, the Château de Losse, the villages of Fanlac, Turenne and Collonges-la-Rouge, and the gardens of Terrasson.*

## Sites open to visitors between Rouffignac and Saint-Léon-sur-Vézère

The **Cent Mammouths** cave, tel. : 05. 53. 05. 41. 71.
**Conquil** prehistoric site, tel. : 05. 53. 51. 29. 03.
**Rouffignac** Tourist Bureau, tel. : 05. 53. 05. 39. 03.

*Other visits: the châteaux of Herm and Fleurac and the charming village of Saint-Léon-sur-Vézère*

## Around Montignac-Lascaux

Route 1

### Following the river Vézère, above Lascaux: La Badegoule

The river Vézère enters Périgord at Terrasson. Above the town, the La Roche-Libère site, which stretches over 2 kilometres (about 1 mile), was already inhabited in prehistoric times. This immense oppidum from the Bronze Age was also inhabited during the Gallic and Roman epochs. One discovers walls 2 metres thick (6 ft.), stone shelters, a tower base, a natural circus which could have been used as an arena. One could think that it is one of the oldest towns in Europe.

In Terrasson, the Lachaud shelter has produced tools dating from the end of the Solutrean age and the Magdalenian. The Jolivet shelter, discovered in 1927, is an example of the main Magdalenian phases. Near Condat, the three rock shelters of Badegoule, excavated as early as 1884 by Jouannet and then by Peyrony, enclose an important Solutrean site. Among the many tools found there, there are very fine "laurel leaf" flints. The presence of tools dating from the early Magdalenian era has made it possible to distinguish a different phase: the Badegoulian (about 16,000 B.C.). The neighbouring site of Machonie dates back to the Aurignacian.

Further north, in Villac, the Sudrie cave has three drawings: including a hind from between the Périgordian and early Magdalenian eras.

*French President Mitterrand in Lascaux for the commemoration of the fiftieth anniversary of the discovery of the cave.*

*Filming of Maurice Bunio's "Children of Lascaux" in Périgord Noir.*
*Above, Abbé Breuil and the schoolteacher Laval at the entrance to the cave and, below, the sequence where Abbé Breuil and the teacher, together with the young discoverers, inaugurate Lascaux in the autumn of 1940.*

*French President Mitterrand giving the commemoration speech at Lascaux in 1990.*

## Into Corrèze, from Turenne to Brive

In Corrèze, between Turenne and Brive, the Noailles cave has produced a type of burin which is characteristic of the Upper Perigordian. South of Noailles, the La Fage chasm, with its beautiful coloured concretions, can be visited. It is full of prehistoric remains from the Chalcolithic era and the Hallstat epoch, and also has a palaeontology museum. To the north of Noailles, one finds the Lamouroux caves, a huge troglodyte village with 80 chambers on five levels, already inhabited in prehistoric times. Further north, the Saint-Antoine caves are of the same type. The decorated caves of Puy-Jarrige, at Brive, and the Moulin de Laguenay, at Chasteaux, are not open to the public. Brive represents an impressive ensemble of caves. Those of Dufour, Bos-del-Ser, Bassaler and Font-Yves demonstrate the transition between Châtelperronian and Aurignacian, while the Font Robert cave held characteristic points. Further east, the Pré-Aubert site, the Coumba-del-Bouïtou cave and the Raysse shelter are characterized by Noailles burins, just like the Esclauzur cave at Larche, where fine Magdalenian spears were found. Study of the Puy-de-Lacan cave at Malemort contributed greatly to our knowledge of the Magdalenian era.

*The real discoverers of Lascaux during the commemoration of the fiftieth anniversary of the inauguration of the cave, at Montignac.*

## Lascaux, the school of the human spirit

Montignac is a small town of 3,000 inhabitants, on the banks of the river Vézère, and owes its fame to the discovery of the eighth wonder of the world in 1940; the Lascaux cave. It is isolated, set apart from the main Palaeolithic population centres, such as Les Eyzies or Castelmerle, just a few kilometres from Montignac, and evokes the mystic splendours of Chartres cathedral, far from the sounds of the city.

Its unexpected discovery sounds like a fairy-tale. On September 12th 1940, four youths decided to explore a hole where their dog had fallen in, on the Lascaux hill. Local legends told of an underground chamber, holding a huge treasure, and linking this spot with Montignac castle. And Marcel Ravidat, Jacques Marsal, C. Agniel and S. Coencas did in fact find a treasure: the Lascaux cave, the most beautiful of all decorated caves from prehistoric times. Experts quarrelled for years about the actual age of Lascaux. These days, prehistorians agree that the paintings date back to the beginning of the Magdalenian era, that is between 16,000 and 15,000 B.C.

Now we shall enter the sanctuary. The very first step into the great Hall of Bulls is amazing. A whirl of animals in movement, with four huge bulls dominating a stampede of horses and deer. All these animals appear to move as one advances deeper into the hall. The prehistoric artists painted them on an imaginary floor line, half way up the wall, and made use of each raised relief of the rock. A calcite chimney gives life to the glance of a deer, a bump turns into a back or a belly, or picks out the muscles of a chest.

The first painting in the hall is intriguing: a panther's skin, a deer's tail, a bison's hump, two horns, this is the famous unicorn both gravid and with a male sex organ. Is it an imaginary animal or, as certain prehistorians timidly suggest, the "sorcerer" of Lascaux, since it has human legs and a face which could have had a muzzle added on. Never forget that, in Prehistory, no explanation can ever be more than a hypothesis.

***Prehistoric artist. Tursac Préhistoparc.***

### The prehistoric palette

*The Palaeolithic artists had found the three fundamental colours of the prehistoric palette in the floor of the cave: manganese dioxide for the black, and iron oxides for the yellow and red ochres, producing many nuances. Excavations have shown how they lit the cave: with a hundred stone lamps containing animal fat. Three painting techniques were employed: drawing, with a finger or crayon, dabbing with tufts of hair or moss, and pulverisation of colour through a hollow bone or blow-pipe, either using a stencil or working directly on the stone.*

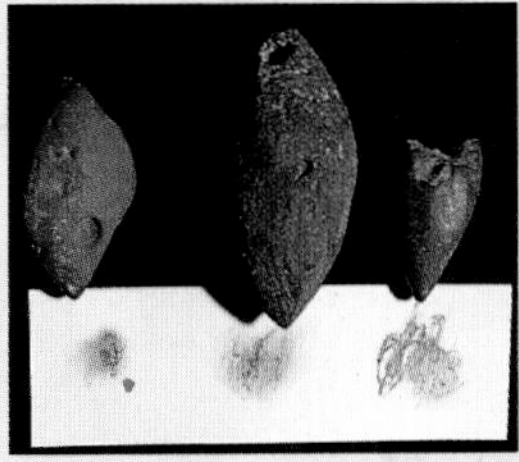

***Palaeolithic "colouring crayons".*** **National Museum of Prehistory at Les Eyzies.**

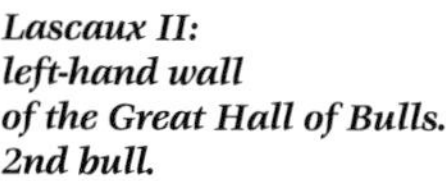

*Lascaux II:
left-hand wall
of the Great Hall of Bulls.
2nd bull.*

*Lascaux II:
head of the great bull,
dating from 17,000 B.C.
and 18 ft. long, the largest
prehistoric painting
known, and the emblem
of Périgord.*

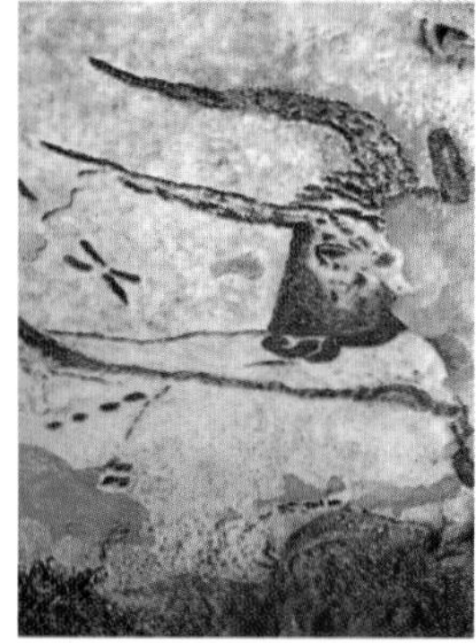

*Lascaux II:
red cow with a black head.*

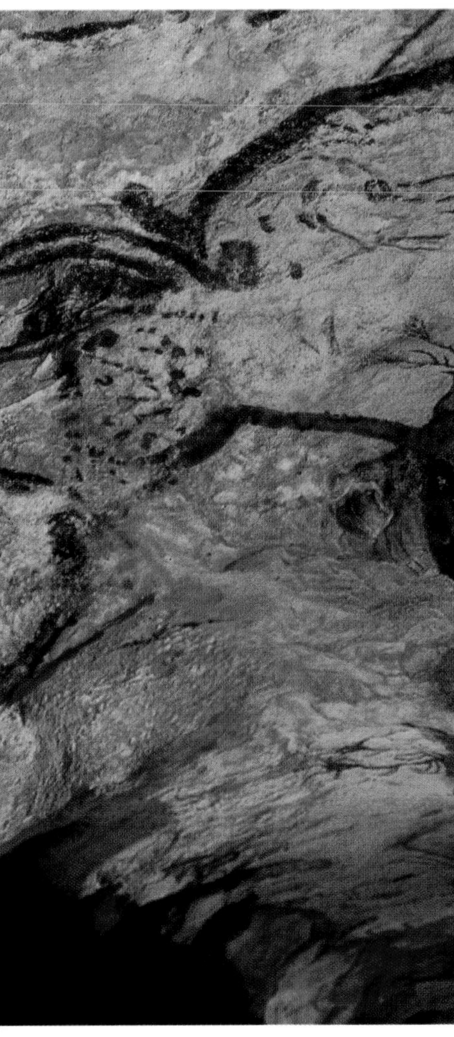

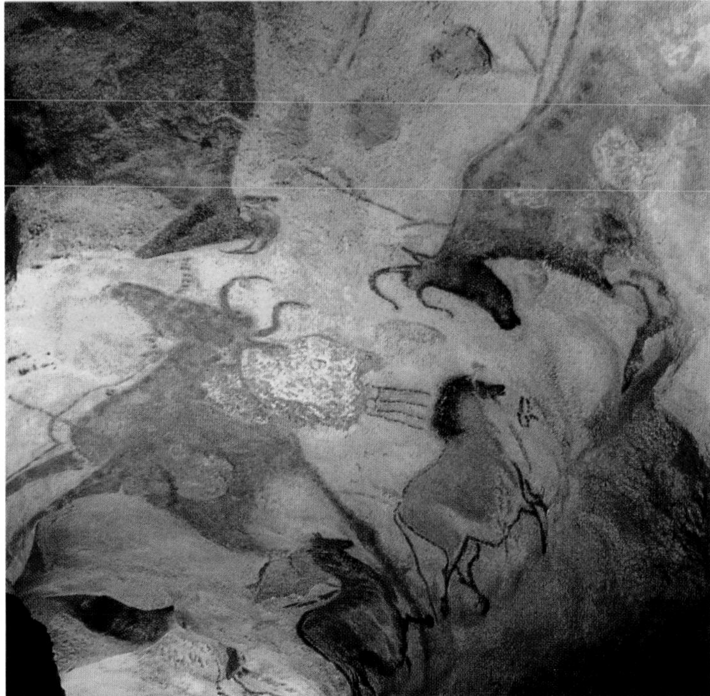

But we must concentrate on these four bulls. In fact, they are aurochs, a race which disappeared from France in the Middle Ages. These enormous paintings - one of them is five and a half metres (18 ft.) - give the hall an impression of life and power. This "presence" is achieved by the technique of turned profile, an artistic effect which depicts the animals in profile and their horns turned by three quarters. This technique, used throughout the Upper Palaeolithic, is not due to the incompetence of the artists but, to the contrary, shows their great ability in representing life.

Facing the entrance a narrow passage opens up, the axial gallery, where one finds the most beautiful paintings of the cave and a painted ceiling, which earned it the title of the "Sistine Chapel of Prehistory", given by Abbé Breuil. Here, the painters were not systematically looking for realism but created genuine compositions, such as this "bouquet" of red cows whose heads form a circle. The two main figures in the passage face each other: a powerful black bull which reminds one of Cretan art and a cow which seems to be jumping in front of a grid traced at its feet.

*Lascaux II: ceiling of the axial gallery and its "bouquet" of red cows. The "Sistine Chapel" of Prehistory.*

*Lascaux II: horses in the axial gallery, right-hand wall.*

*Lascaux II: the unicorn (8 ft. long) on the left-hand wall of the Hall of Bulls.*

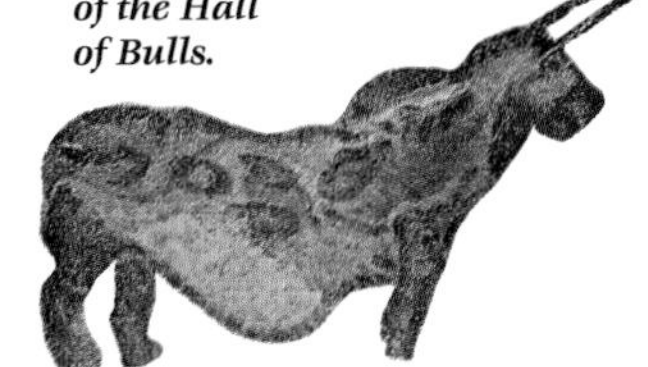

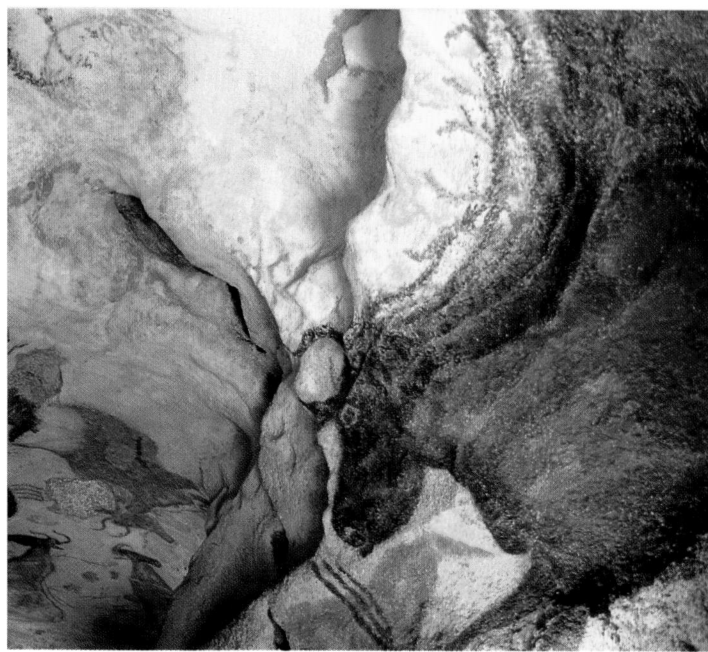

*Lascaux II: axial gallery: "Cretan" bull.*

The horse is present in many forms. The well-known "Chinese horse", stylized, allows us to appreciate the technique of the artists better. The belly, partly covered in ochre, is rounded. In the background, the hoofs, separated from the body, create a perspective effect. This technique was only rediscovered at the time of the Renaissance. At the end of the gallery, a very realistic horse gallops with its mane blowing in the wind, while its twin, or double, falls down with its legs in the air. It could be a hunting scene where the horses are frightened by men and jump off the top of a cliff.

*Lascaux II: "Chinese" horse.*

Returning to the great hall and taking the second passage on the left, one reaches the nave, a vast cavity where the paintings have suffered the ravages of time more than elsewhere. A big black cow dominates the scene by its

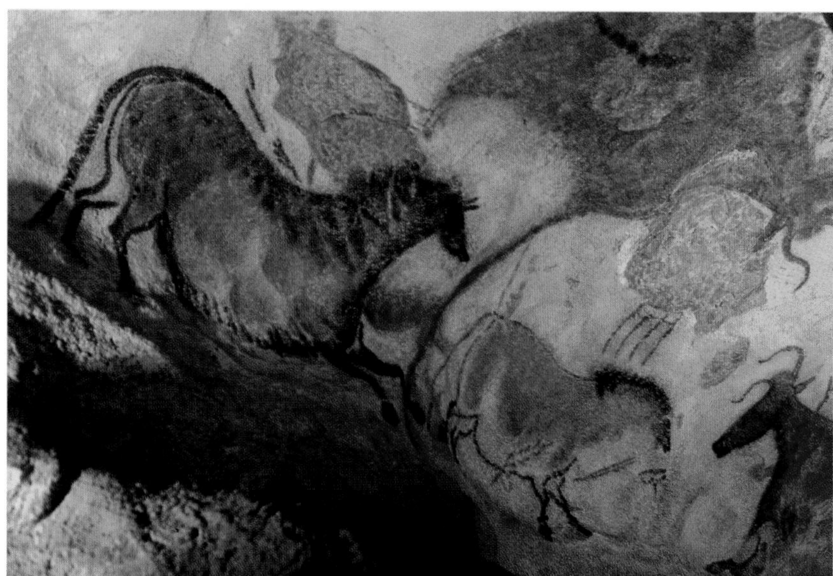

*Lascaux II: Chinese horses: right-hand wall of the axial gallery.*

size, while two bison, remarkable through their savage force and blind frenzy, run away as if surprised by the visitor's regard.

On the other side, a frieze of five deer which seem to be swimming offers a gentler image. There is a passage which is difficult to enter and which leads to a little room containing several engravings, mostly feline. Finally, a recess in the nave, the apse, with walls covered by a multitude of engravings, opens onto a well. Four metres (13 ft.) lower down, this well holds yet another enigma: what meaning should be given to this wounded bison losing its entrails, this rhinoceros, this bird perched on a stick and this naked man, ithyphallic, drawn in a childish way?

***Lascaux II:***
***"falling horse" and small horse's head at the end of the axial gallery.***

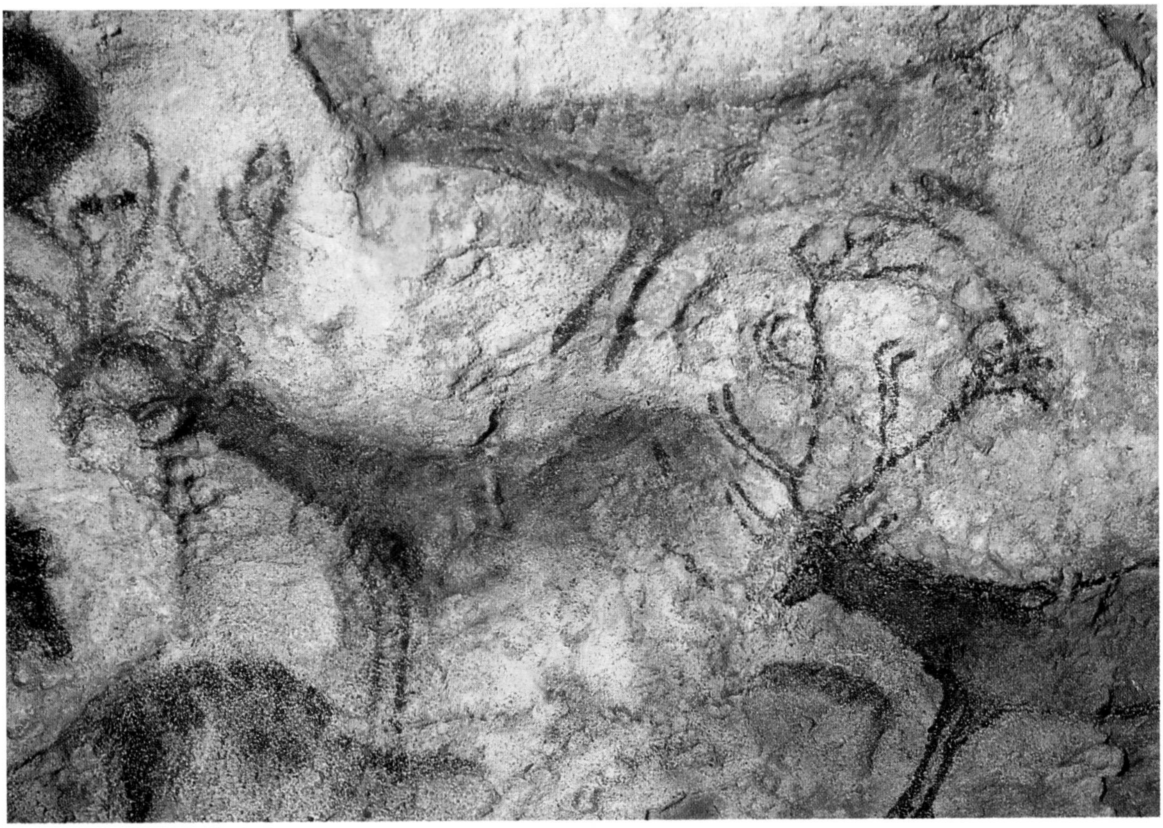

***Lascaux II:***
***left-hand wall of the Great Hall: frieze of small deer.***

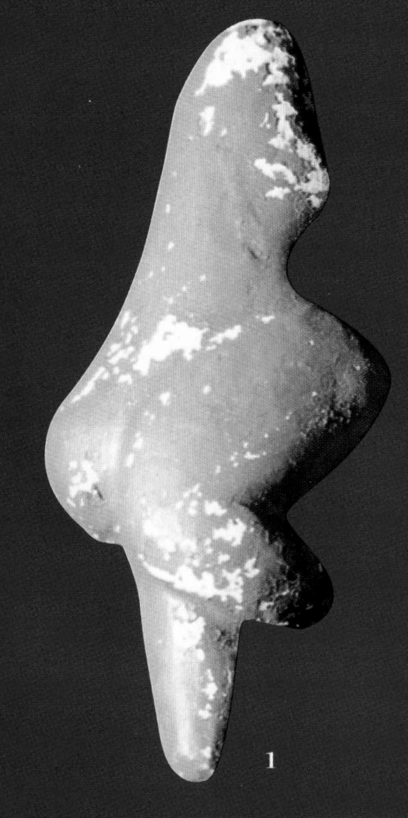

1

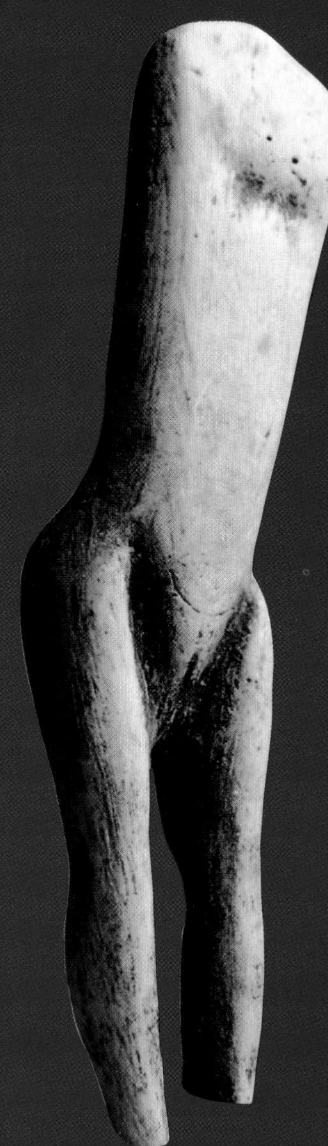

2

## *Mysterious human forms*

*Representations of man are always deformed. The male images are usually deliberately clumsy and sometimes of half-human or half-animal form. The female images, more frequent, are obese statuettes, with enormous breasts and hips, interpreted as fertility symbols. They are generally very old (25,000 B.C.) and are generically termed "Venuses".*

3

4

5

*1 - Mould of the "Tursac Venus", calcite statuette (3 1/4 in. x 1 1/2 in.) found in the Facteur shelter. It possibly dates from the later Perigordian.* **National Museum of Prehistory at Les Eyzies.**

*2 - Mould of the "Immodest Venus", statuette in mammoth tusk (3 1/4 in.) found in Laugerie-Basse, at Les Eyzies. Dating imprecise (Magdalenian). The first prehistoric statuette to be discovered in France (1864).* Photo J.-G. Marcillaud.

*3 - Bison head and human silhouettes engraved on a rib fragment of a large herbivorous animal, the so-called Raymonden "bison plate", late Magdalenian.* **Périgord Museum, Périgueux.**

*4 - Mould of the "Sireuil Venus", calcite statuette (3 3/4 in. x 2 in.), found in the Sireuil cave. Perigordian.* **National Museum of Prehistory at Les Eyzies.**

*5 - Mould of the Venus found in 1958 in the Pataud shelter. End of Perigordian or Perigordian VI.* **National Museum of Prehistory at Les Eyzies.**

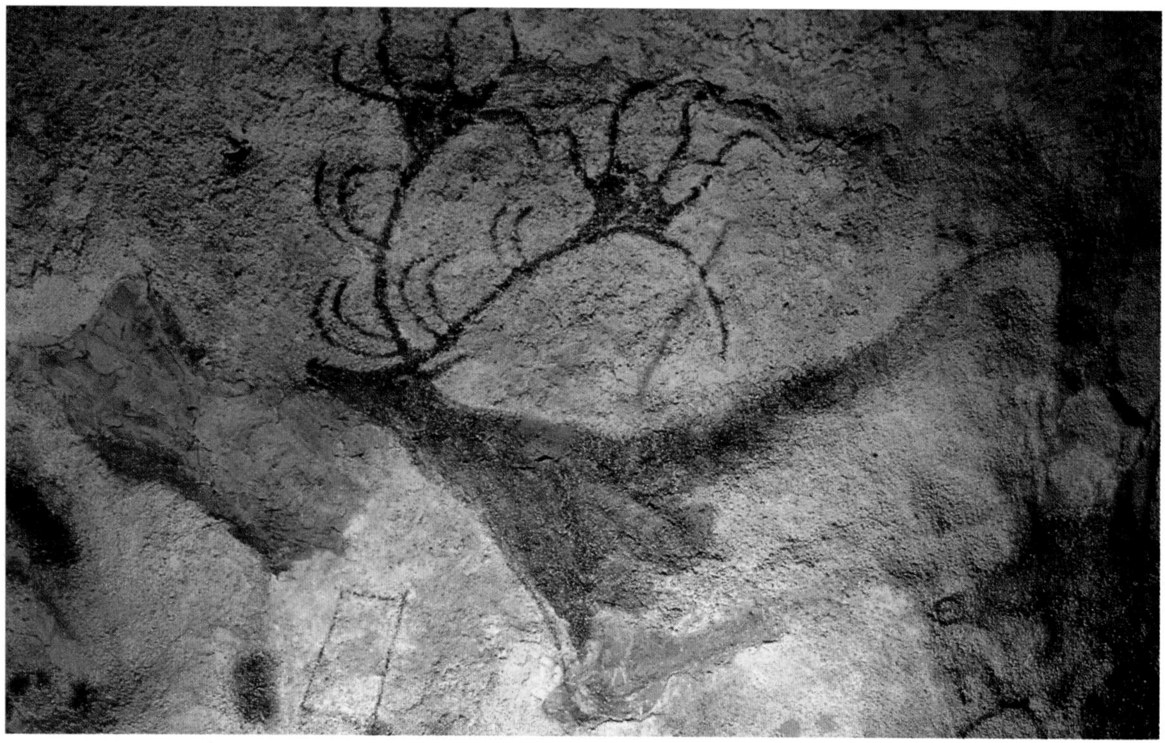

***Lascaux II:* deer's head on the right-hand side of the axial gallery.**

## Prehistoric art

This famous ensemble leads us to think about the meaning of cave wall art which probably appeared in the Aurignacian period, 30,000 B.C. at the epoch when Cro-Magnon man "succeeded" Neanderthal man. From its origins until the decadence of the art at the end of the Magdalenian period, about 9,000 B.C., artists repeated the same themes in a stable geographical region, from the Urals to the Atlantic. They reached the peak of their art between 18,000 and 10,000 B.C. with the decorated caves of the south-west of France and the north-west of Spain. Therefore one can talk about a real prehistoric civilization without knowing whether it had the slightest political or social unity, but which used the same technique of carved stone, the same culture and, probably, the same religion.

Périgord was at the centre of this prehistoric world, which is why one can say that if Africa was the cradle of humanity, Périgord saw the birth of art. Cro-Magnon man and his successors were not at all brutes wearing animal skins, as they are so often depicted. They were men in their own right, and in no way inferior to man of today.

But prehistoric paintings remain a mystery. The first prehistorians, referring to examples of present-day primitives, talk about hunting or fertility rites. In his book *Religions of Prehistory* (P.U.F.), André Leroi-Gourhan notes that the paintings are always statistically arranged in the same order and concludes that this is a sort of message based on male and female symbols, which one cannot interpret. The fact that drawings are often found at the bottom of caves or on the edges of chasms can allow one to put forward the hypothesis of an earth religion, mother of all life. But the symbolic study of prehistoric art is still to be made.

We can only conclude that the emotion we feel when we see these decorated walls was also felt by prehistoric man. In this way, we are very close to him.

## Lascaux II, a prehistoric chef-d'œuvre of the XXth century

Although it was miraculously preserved by a totally impermeable layer of clay, Lascaux was later attacked on two fronts by illnesses brought from outside by visitors: first of all the "green leprosy", a proliferation of algae, and then the "white disease", an accelerated formation of calcite. In 1963, the cave was closed to the public. After being given specialized treatment like a seriously ill patient, it has now recovered its former brilliance, but it can never again open its doors to the public without risk of a relapse.

It took ten years of work to constitute Lascaux II, a facsimile, under the auspices of the Departmental Tourist Board,

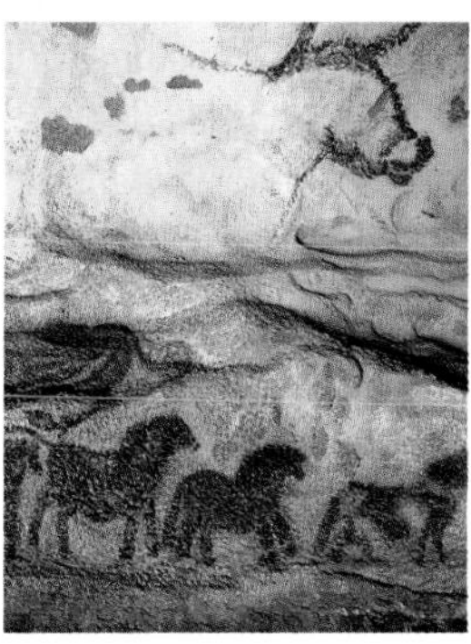

***Lascaux II:* *frieze of little horses, axial gallery, right-hand wall.***

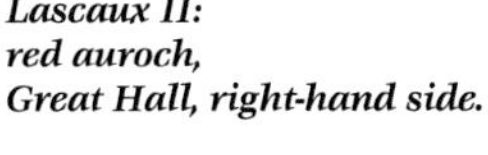

***Lascaux II:* *red auroch, Great Hall, right-hand side.***

*The Régourdou site, at Montignac.*

*Top right: Régourdou bear.*

*Opposite page: Top: Le Thot, re-created prehistoric habitat.*

*Bottom left: Le Thot: articulated mammoth.*

*Bottom right: Le Thot: re-creation of a prehistoric hut in mammoth bones, discovered in Siberia.*

together with the Dordogne General Council. Daniel Debaye was in charge of the work and many artists took part in the operation. The computers of these days made it possible for Renaud Sanson to re-create the volumes to the very millimetre. The paintings, using natural pigments and prehistoric techniques, were the work of Monique Peytral. The facsimile is a chef-d'œuvre in itself. Only a specialist could say that he was not in the real cave. The entry chamber has been transformed into a museum. Even though only the great hall and the axial gallery have been reproduced, you cannot miss the most beautiful of all the prehistoric decorated caves we know today.

## Le Régourdou and the bear cult

A few hundred metres from Lascaux, but 55,000 years earlier, the prehistoric site of Régourdou, open for visits, perplexes prehistorians. When he was looking for another entrance to the Lascaux cave, Roger Constant discovered a tomb surrounded by dry-stone walls containing a Neanderthal skeleton with many bear bones. This discovery, in 1954, was the basis of the often-contested theory of the bear cult in the Mousterian age. There is a small museum on the site. On the other slope, one finds the Balutie cave, inhabited between the Aurignacian and Magdalenian eras.

*Roger Constant shows his finds: Régourdou man (femur and jaw-bone).*

## Thonac and the Thot Centre of Prehistoric Art

From the village of Thonac, one can see the prehistoric site of Maillol, the Croze de Salvetou cave with its scratches and inscriptions, and that of the Batusserie, with its prehistoric engravings studied by Abbé Glory. Twenty-seven axes from the bronze age were found in Thonac.

One kilometre, or half a mile, to the north, the Thot Prehistoric Centre is open to visitors. It was built in 1972, under the auspices of the Departmental Tourist Office, and is an excellent introduction to Prehistory. There is a zoological park representing the "survivors of prehistoric fauna" - bison, tarpan horses, deer, aurochs, Przewalski horses - with films and panoramic slide projections showing the techniques of the Paleolithic artists, and moulds of objects such as a mammoth and an articulated rhinoceros. The visit is fascinating for both adults and children.

*Thot deer*

*Lascaux II: Deer (28 in.) left-hand side of the Great Hall.*

## PREHISTORIC BESTIARY

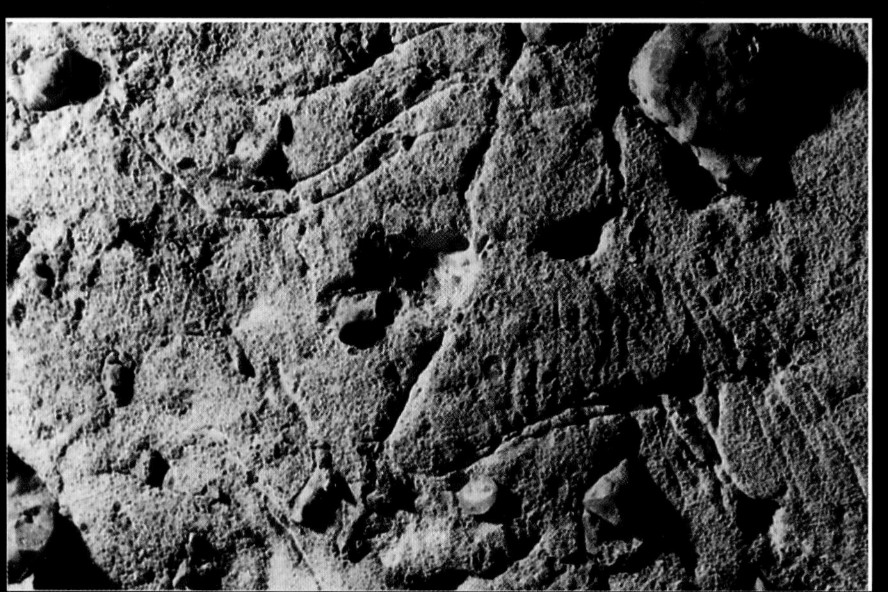

*Bara-Bahau (Le Bugue) auroch drawn in deep lines in the soft rock.*

*Right: Still there! (Le Thot)*

*European bison at Le Thot.*

*This bison licking his flanks is carved on a spear thrower made of reindeer horn. It is a fine example of portable art left by the inhabitants of La Madeleine. Mould at the National Museum of Prehistory, Les Eyzies.*

*Tarpan horse, Le Thot.*

*Lascaux II: galloping horse.*

## ROUFFIGNAC AND SAINT-LÉON-SUR-VÉZÈRE

Route 2

### Rouffignac-les Cent Mammouths, voyage to the centre of the earth

A short way away from the Vézère valley, 8 kilometres (5 miles) from the river and perched on the heights dividing the waters of the Isle and the Vézère, one finds the Grotte des Cent Mammouths (Hundred Mammoths' Cave), also known under the name of Miremont or Cro de Granville. There are no gas lamps as at the time of Jules Verne, but a little electric train. This vast cave, with more than eight kilometres (five miles) of galleries,

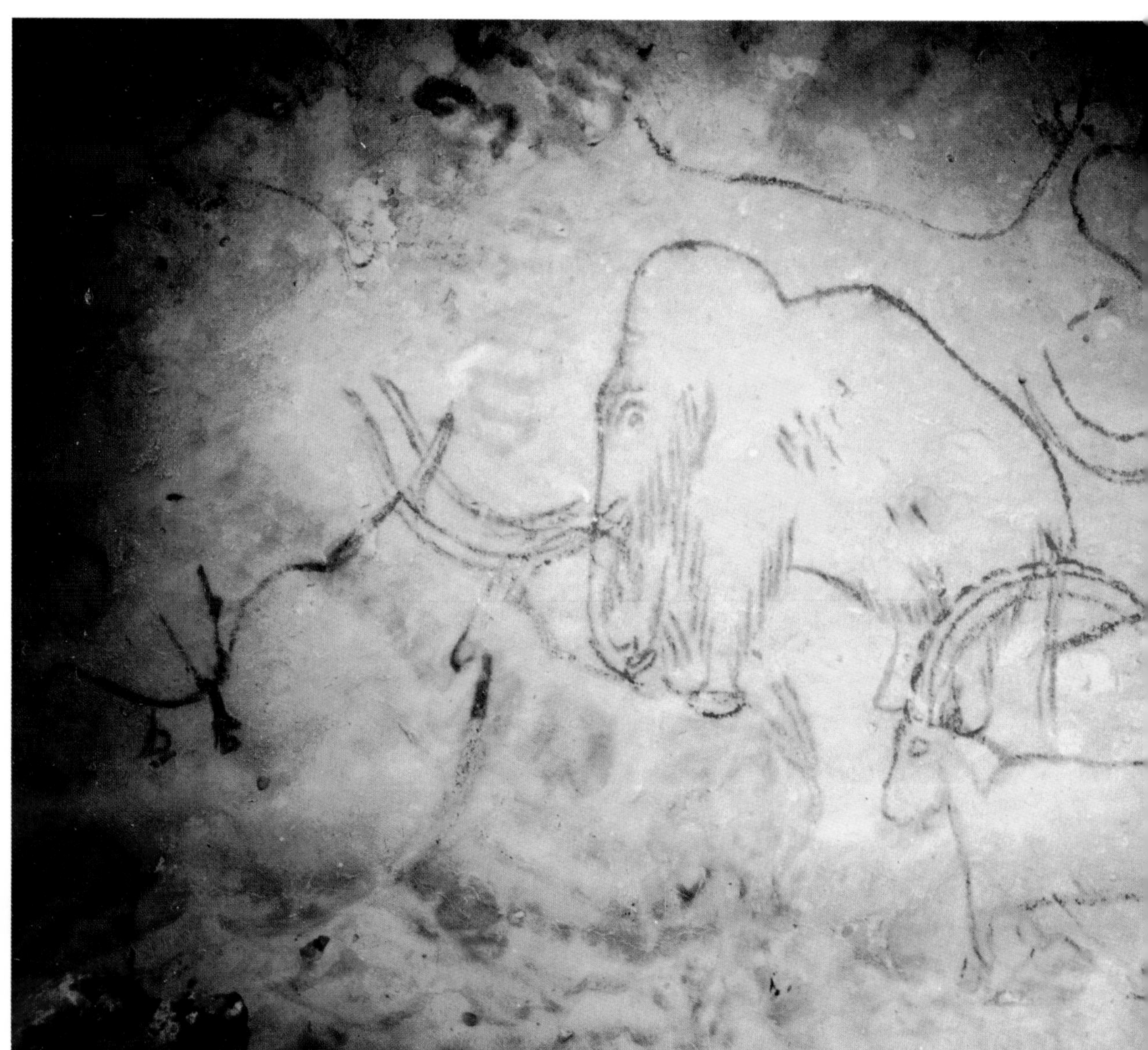

***Rouffignac: mammoth and ibex on the huge ceiling of the Hundred-Mammoths cave.*** Photo Éditions la Goélette, Paris.

has never been closed and has been receiving visitors since the XVIth century. Even though it had been explored by illustrious prehistorians such as Martel, Breuil and Glory, its paintings were only discovered in 1956, by Nougier and Robert. Although there were many who claimed they were a hoax at the time, no-one doubts their authenticity these days. This cave was occupied in recent times. The paintings date from the middle and upper Magdalenian, or 11,000 B.C. Excavations at the mouth of the cave have revealed traces of human occupation at the end of prehistoric times (Tardenoisian man, Sauveterrian, Neolithic and the iron age). Long before any art appeared, man must have been fighting the bears for possession of these caverns; lairs and traces of claw marks are still there as evidence of their presence.

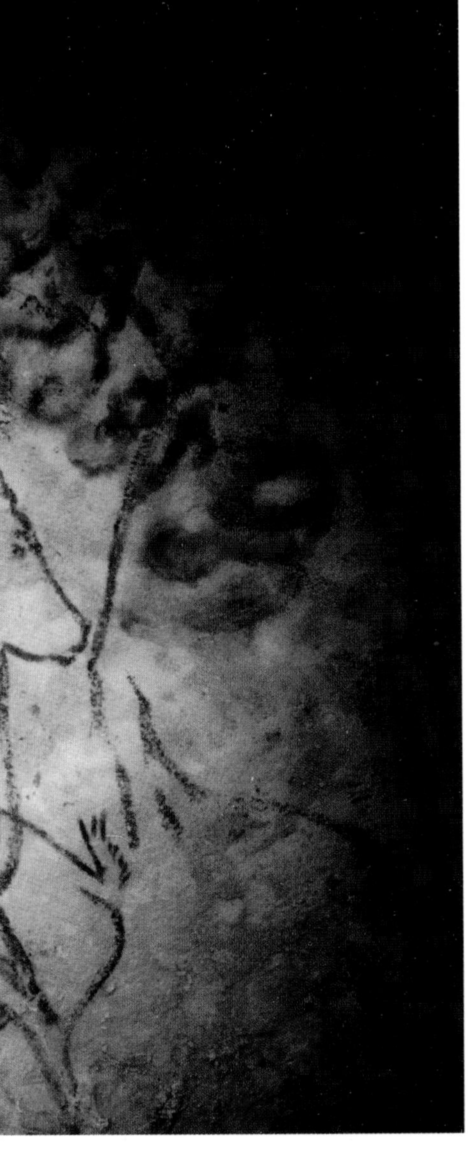

The first engravings are found 800 metres from the entrance, and they continue until the end of the galleries. There are lines traced out by fingers in this very soft rock, called "meanders" or "macaroni" and which are characteristic of this cave. They can easily be distinguished from more recent graffiti since they are covered with a greyish patina which Abbé Breuil called the "dirt of ages". The mammoth is

## The mammoth in cave wall art

*The cave owes its name to the number of figures of mammoths it contains, about 150. It alone contains half of the representations of this animal known, a phenomenon which is quite out of the ordinary since the mammoth is generally a secondary subject in cave wall art. In total, it only makes up 8% of figures, far behind the horse and horned cattle, 30% each. The latter are always placed in the centre of compositions, a fact which enabled A. Leroi-Gourhan to work out a theory of symbolism linked with prehistoric art. It is also curious to note that this mammoth sanctuary dates from an epoch when the animal was in the process of disappearing from our regions, like the woolly rhinoceros which can be admired in a frieze there.*

**Rouffignac: woolly rhinocerus. Like its contemporary, the mammoth, it haunted our lands before disappearing around 10,000 B.C.**
Photo Éditions la Goélette, Paris.

***Among the first engraved animals from Prehistory: capridae on a Belcayre stone slab (Thonac, Aurignacian I) from around 30,000 B.C.***
**National Museum of Prehistory at Les Eyzies.**

***Demonstration of a spear thrower. Le Conquil.***
Photo L. Roulland.

sometimes represented very realistically, such as the famous "patriarch" with his back marked by ritual signs, but generally speaking only the outline is traced out. Near a sink-hole, the artist has drawn two herds clashing. The little train stops at the mouth of the great hall whose painted ceiling, a composition of horses, bison, ibex and mammoths, is the chef-d'œuvre of Rouffignac. This hall is on the edge of a chasm. The drawing and the chasm are associated ten times in the cave. This is too much for sheer hazard, and the fact that paintings have been found in places which are difficult to reach, and also dangerous, is an argument in favour of a religion based on the hidden forces of the earth. Just as at Lascaux, representations of human figures have been discovered at the edge of these chasms which lead to a lower level of the cave, where four kilometres (2.5 miles) of galleries have already been explored.

The huge dolmen of Rouffignac dates back to more recent prehistoric times, at Le Cayre. According to local legend, the dolmen goes every night to drink in the waters of a nearby fountain, at Fontfarge.

Not far away, at Fleurac, there is a deposit of bronze axes. Near Plazac, in the Maurélie cave, bronze age pottery has been found.

## Saint-Léon-sur-Vézère: Belcayre and Conquil

Between Thonac and Saint-Léon-sur-Vézère, the elegant Renaissance château of Belcayre holds important prehistoric remains. The site of Balcayre-Haut, discovered in 1875, was occupied in the Aurignacian period. Below the château is the rock shelter of La Rochette (or Belcayre-Bas). Although it was inhabited in the Mousterian and Châtelperronian periods, it dates mainly from the Aurignacian and Perigordian times. The Renne shelter contained a stone slab engraved with an ibex dating from the Aurignacian period. The neighbouring Métairie shelter revealed Mousterian remains, Aurigignacian blades, spears and jewellery, and Magdalenian tools.

At Saint-Léon, on the left bank of the Vézère, the Conquil site, open to visitors, is an ensemble of natural troglodyte habitats occupied in prehistoric and Gallo-Roman times, and in the Middle Ages. Apart from a superb walk in enchanting surroundings, the visitor can learn how to sharpen flints and to use a prehistoric bow and arrow or a spear-thrower.

*Le Conquil.*
*Top left:*
*Fortified halls.*
Photo L. Roulland.

*Troglodyte natural park: the "pigeon house" which could have been a temple to Mithra. Le Conquil.*
Photo L. Roulland.

*Demonstration of chipping flints. Le Conquil.*
Photo L. Roulland.

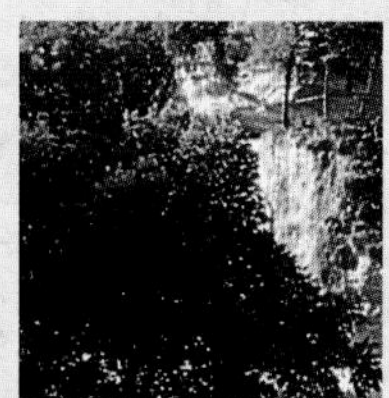

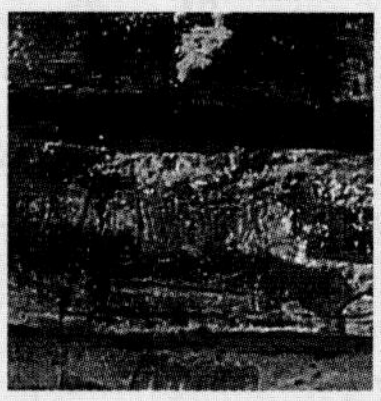

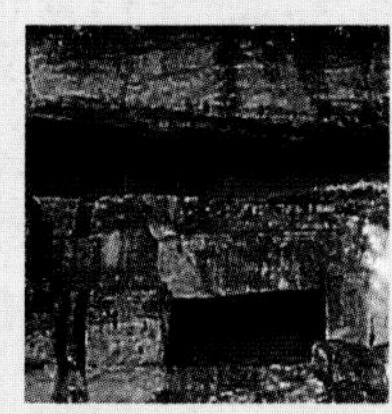

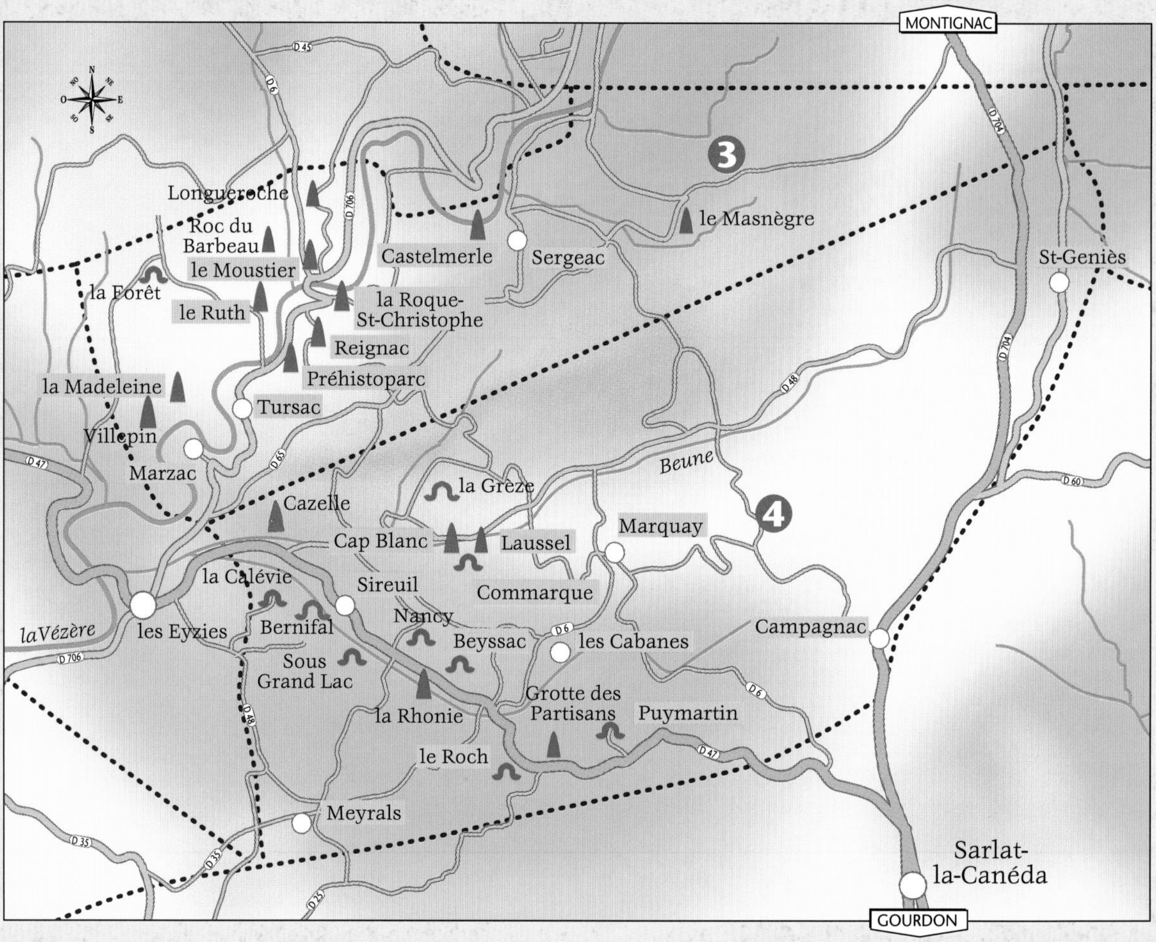

MONTIGNAC
D 45
D 6
D 706
D 704
3
Longueroche
Roc du
Barbeau
le Moustier
la Forêt
le Ruth
Castelmerle
Sergeac
le Masnègre
St-Geniès
la Roque-
St-Christophe
Reignac
Préhistoparc
la Madeleine
Tursac
Villepin
Marzac
D 47
D 65
D 48
Beune
D 60
4
la Grèze
Cazelle
Cap Blanc
Laussel
Marquay
Commarque
la Calévie
Sireuil
les Eyzies
laVézère
D 706
Bernifal
Nancy
Beyssac
D 6
les Cabanes
Campagnac
Sous
Grand Lac
la Rhonie
Grotte des
Partisans
Puymartin
D 6
D 47
D 48
le Roch
Meyrals
D 35
D 35
D 25
Sarlat-
la-Canéda
GOURDON

Prehistoric cave, decorated or with concretions, open to the public.
Prehistoric site open to the public.
Decorated Prehistoric cave (not open to the public).
Other Prehistoric site.
Megalith.
Museum with Prehistoric collections.
Laussel Site or locality with interesting prehistoric sites.
Sergeac Non-Prehistoric tourist site.
3 Route number.
Route described in this book.

0 2 4 km

Mapping by ACTUAL

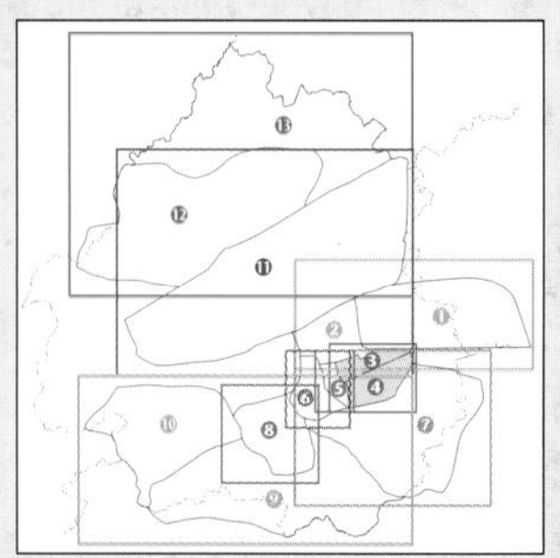

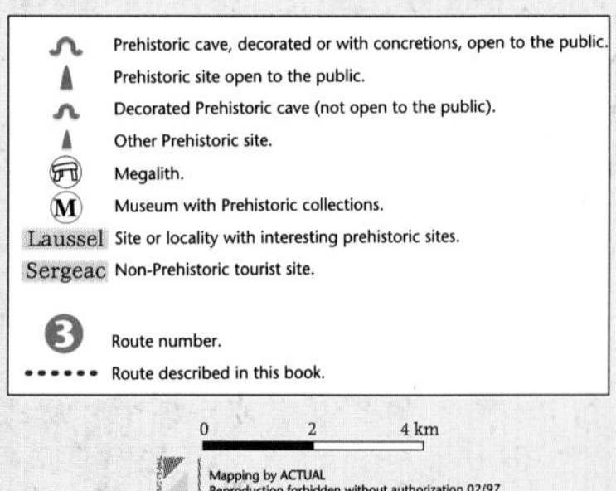

# From Les Eyzies
## to Sergeac or to Sarlat

### Following the river Vézère, between Sergeac and les Eyzies

Route 3

#### Sergeac-Castelmerle

We shall continue our descent of the Vézère river to reach the Knights Templar village of Sergeac which has revealed important prehistoric remains.

A little to the west of the village, in the vale of Castelmerle (or the Roches vale) there are rock shelters open to the public. After Les Eyzies, this was the most densely populated area in the Périgord Noir in the Palaeolithic era. Its nine shelters were inhabited between 50,000 and 10,000 B.C. and many works of art and tools have been found here. The Blanchard I shelter, inhabited in

***Engraved horse, Reverdit shelter. Castelmerle.***
Photo A. Bordes.

### Sites open to visitors between Sergeac and Tursac

***Castelmerle*** *(9 rock shelters), tel. 05.53.50.79.70 or 05.53.50.74.79. and the Castanet museum*
***Le Moustier*** *shelter, tel. 05.53.06.90.80.*
***La Roque-Saint-Christophe Fort****, tel. 05.53.50.70.45.*
***Reignac*** *stronghold*
***La Madeleine Fort****, tel. 05.53.06.92.49.*
***Ruth hamlet*** *(Cellier and Pagès shelters), tel. 05.53.50.74.02.*
***Préhistoparc****, tel. 05.53.50.73.19.*

*All these sites are linked by the GR 36 which allows one to discover on foot the extraordinary landscapes of the Vézère cliffs. Do not miss the Knights Templar village of Sergeac, the Marzac and Chaban châteaux, the site of the côte de Jor and its Buddhist monastery.*

### Sites open to visitors in the valley of the Beunes

***Bernifal*** *cave, tel. 05.53.29.66.39.*
***La Rhone fort****, tel. 05.53.29.24.83.*
***Cap-Blanc*** *sculpted rock shelter, tel. 05.53.59.21.74 and 05.53.29.66.63.*
***La Grèze*** *cave*

*The GR 6 which links Sarlat to Les Eyzies following the Beunes reveals the remarkable site of Commarque castle with its medieval ruined village. One can also visit the castles of Puymartin and Campagnac and the village of Saint Geniès.*

*Castelmerle*
***Above: La Souquette shelter;***
***Below: bear head, Reverdit shelter.***
***Right: carved frieze, Reverdit shelter;***
Photos A. Bordes.

the Aurignacian period (30,000 to 25,000 years B.C.) discovered in 1910 and then studied by Abbé Breuil, has revealed twenty stone blocks with animal engravings, sometimes covered with paintings, as well as ringed and cupped blocks. These works of art are among humanity's most ancient. The adjacent Castanet shelter, investigated by Peyrony, presents the same features. The Labattut shelter, excavated in 1912 and then studied by Breuil and Glory, was inhabited in the Gravettian and Solutrean periods. The skeleton of a child, dating back to the latter period, was found there. There were also paintings, two stone slabs engraved with animals and ringed blocks, works of art from the Perigordian epoch. The Labattut shelter retains traces of a hearth and a workshop for carving flints. One can see reproductions of the paintings and engravings which decorated the ceiling of the rock shelter 20,000 years ago.

The Reverdit shelter, discovered in 1878, was excavated by Breuil, Capitan and Peyrony. It shows five animals sculpted in low-relief from the Magdalenian period. There are also strange

*Moustier rock shelter,*
***The Mousterian period is named after this site.***

symbols, from 32,000 years ago. The Souquette shelter, the habitat of Cro-Magnon hunters, has given up many remains of bones and tools. It was occupied from the Aurignacian period (35,000 B.C.) until our day. The Roc d'Acier is an example of Perigordian and Solutrean habitats.

The vale of Castelmerle also holds the Blanchard II and Merveilles shelters, frequented in the Mousterian era and then in the Gravettian, as well as the Roches shelter. The Castanet museum, situated above the site, displays discoveries from these various prehistoric sites. The enormous number of discoveries made on this site lead us to think about these famous carved stones. We shall not describe all the different techniques for cutting the blades, but as time passed certain tools became sharper and more varied, as Leroi-Gourhan demonstrates in his book *The Hunters of Prehistory* (A.-M. Métaillé).

At Castelmerle, which Abbé Breuil appreciated so much, one can visit the Reverdit shelter at the same time as the troglodyte stronghold called the "Fort of the English", perhaps inhabited in Prehistoric times, but where an important *cluzeau*, or shelter dug out of the cliff, was added in the Middle Ages. Although its dimensions are fairly small, the fort combined habitat, fortifications and a system of defence.

## Peyzac-Le Moustier

Peyzac and Le Moustier are two villages on either side of the river Vézère. On the left bank: Peyzac, on the right bank Le Moustier. Prehistory, omnipre-

### Mousterian

*Several human types, grouped together under the general term of Paleanthropians, cohabited at this epoch, but the best known and the most widely spread was Neanderthal Man. This man, whose physical aspect appears somewhat animal-like to us, nonetheless had a cranial capacity which was larger than our own. He had abstract ideas, since he buried his dead, used colours, and collected fossils and shells. One knows that he took special care of his burial places. Although Neanderthal man disappeared fairly rapidly after the "appearance" of Homo sapiens sapiens, there was no industrial rupture between the two epochs. Although Mousterian man may not be our direct ancestor genetically, we are incontestably his heirs..., from the cultural and technical point of view.*

sent as in Les Eyzies, has made the commune famous. There are the sites of Jardel, Fongal, the roc du Barbeau (Sauveterrian), Combe de Banc and above all the well-known Moustier rock shelter, open to visitors, which gave its name to the Mousterian period.

There are two rock shelters, excavated successively by Lartet in 1864 and by Peyrony, each presenting Mousterian remains of Acheulian tradition, typical Mousterian covering a period from 100,000 to 35,000 B.C., Châtelperronian, a transition period when modern man appeared, Aurignacian (30,000 B.C.) and early Perigordian. F. Bordes, H. Laville and J.-Ph. Rigaud completed the study of the site.

In the second shelter, in 1908, O. Hauser, (a dealer in antiquity rather than an archeologist) discovered a Neanderthal skeleton, Moustier Man, which he sold to the Berlin Museum.

These terraced caves overlook a wonderful panorama over the Vézère valley. There is a little on-site museum covering the Mousterian period which, for 65,000 years, was geographically significant in Europe, Asia and North Africa.

## La Roque-Saint-Christophe

At the "Pas du Miroir", one kilometre (half a mile) to the west, where the road runs between the cliff and the river and winds its way around the rocks, one can visit La Roque-Saint-Christophe, one of the most extraordinary prehistoric sites of Périgord, overlooking the river Vézère. This remarkable troglodyte stronghold, 80 metres high (265 ft.), 500 metres long (550 yds) and on five levels, is a "must" for anyone interested in Prehistory and archeology. This vast natural terrace, one of the biggest in Europe, was inhabited from the Mousterian epoch (70,000 B.C.). It then sheltered Cro-Magnon men, those from Neolithic times, the Bronze Age (1,500 B.C.) the Iron Age (800 B.C.), Gallo-Roman times and the Middle Ages. The site which the visitor sees today is a gigantic troglodyte ensemble which can only be compared with Cappadoce in Turkey. The troglodyte fort was built by Frotaire, Bishop of Périgueux in the Xth century, to stop the Vikings navigating the Vézère. The latter are supposed to have dug out a channel, to get around the obstacle, but the traces which remain may well be natural. The English took the fort in 1401, massacring all its defenders and, so the story tells, burying a rich treasure. Five years later, the French retook the stronghold. Since the Roque-Saint-Christophe was inhabited by the Huguenots, Henri III had the fortress destroyed in 1588. However, there are still extensive remains to be seen

*The Reignac fortified house shelters a prehistoric site.*

which never fail to amaze visitors.

After crossing the original threshold of the fort, one discovers that the rocks are pitted with thousands of square niches, used for holding the beams which supported the houses. The shelters reveal recipients carved out of the rock, channels for collecting and evacuating water, and also about 1,500 rings carved from the rock, for attaching animals and lamps. Certain halls evidently had a precise purpose (abattoir, smoke-house, safe). The village itself, suspended on five terraces, could house between 1,000 and 1,500 inhabitants. One can imagine the bustle of life, the traders' boutiques, the workshops of the artisans. The church is easily recognisable from its engraved crosses and tombs. A vast panorama over the Vézère opens out from the terrace. On the other side of the valley, one can see a

***Near Moustier, La Roque-Saint-Christophe is one of the biggest natural terraces in Europe.***
Photo J.-M. Touron.

***Opposite page: La Roque-Saint-Christophe: the main staircase.***
Photo J.-M. Touron.

***La Roque-Saint-Christophe, overlooking the river Vézère, one of the most impressive prehistoric and troglodyte sites of Périgord.***
Photo J.-M. Touron.

***Kitchen in the fort. La Roque-Saint-Christophe.***
Photo J.-M. Touron.

***La Roque-Saint-Christophe, huge natural terrace, 570 yards long.***
Photo J.-M. Touron.

*The river Vézère at the foot of La Madeleine, seen from Marzac.*

cave in the cliff: an advance look-out post. The troglodyte strongholds formed a defensive network and probably communicated with each other with sound or light signals. Certain halls have paleochristian and perhaps prehistoric engravings. Others display discoveries made on the site and reconstitutions of Neanderthal men. For safety reasons, it is no longer possible to visit the "Pas du Miroir" where one used to be able to look over to see one's reflection in the waters of the Vézère far below.

By taking a Dantesque road bordered by fallen rocks, which gives the impression that the cliff is about to collapse, one reaches the stronghold of Reignac, one kilometre (half a mile) to the south-west. This is built on a troglodyte dwelling and a prehistoric site. It was inhabited in the Magdalenian era, and then in the Bronze and Iron Ages, and several pieces of art have been found there. It is open to visitors.

## Tursac-La Madeleine, Le Ruth and Préhistoparc

***La Madeleine Shelter and Fort***

With its XIIth century fortified Romanesque church, a belltower keep and a row of domes, and its carved stone cross, the little village of Tursac is one of Périgord's principal prehistoric centres. Opposite the village, on the right bank of the Vézère in beautiful surroundings for the walker, at water-level, is the huge rock shelter of La Madeleine, which gave its name to the Magdalenian period. Excavations were started there in 1863 by Lartet and continued by Peyrony, and revealed a large range of tools, fine specimens of portable art and a child's skeleton. Above all, they established the entire chronology from the Middle Magdalenian to the Upper Magdalenian, since the site was occupied until the Azilian period, that is 12,000 - 8,000 B.C.

The prehistoric part of La Madeleine is not open to the general public, but no-one will regret this visit to the troglodyte fort and the remains of the

***La Madeleine (Tursac): troglodyte shelter and chapel.***

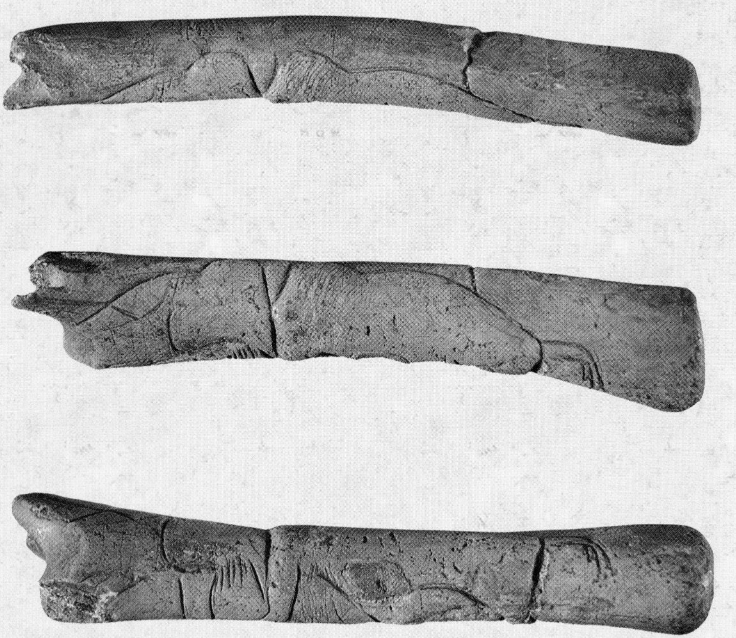

***Confronting mammoths on perforated sticks made of reindeer horn from Laugerie-Haute, early Magdalenian, about 22,000 years old.*** **National Museum of Prehistory at Les Eyzies.**

## Magdalenian

*The Magdalenian era, between 15,000 B.C. and 9,000 B.C. is the last great phase of the Upper Palaeolithic. After this, art entered a period of decadence. This is the epoch when most of the great cave paintings were produced: Lascaux, Font-de-Gaume, Rouffignac, and also Altamira, Niaux, Pech-Merle. Man had introduced the idea of «beauty» into his daily life, decorating the objects he used (spears, spear-throwers, perforated sticks), working bone and wood, and creating portable art of very fine quality. His tools were very varied and specialized (burins, harpoons, scrapers, spear-throwers). We do not know what some of these tools were used for.*

castle. From the parking place, it is recommended to take the little path through the woods, which is cared for, and which leads to the site of La Madeleine. Here, as in many places in Périgord, one finds a village from the Middle Ages (Xth century) added to the original prehistoric site, carved into the rock and fortified to resist the raids of the Vikings. In this vast troglodyte village, which was still inhabited in the XVIIth century, one notes a XVth century chapel, which local legend says hides a treasure, and an "aerial cluzeau" or "look-out cabin" dug out of the cliff. By walking around, one can understand the defence system of the village and the daily life of our troglodyte ancestors. The hill is topped by the medieval castle of Petit Marzac, the third level of this fine example of the pereniality of life through the centuries and millennia. The castle, built between the XIVth and XVIth centuries, is now in ruins on its rocky promontory, but it still stands proudly with its thick walls pierced by its mullion windows, its curtain walls and its circular tower.

A hundred metres away from the La Madeleine rock shelter stands the Villepin shelter, excavated in 1917 by Peyrony. It was inhabited between the end of the Magdalenian era and the Azilian period (10,000 - 8,000 B.C.).

### *Ruth hamlet: the Cellier and Pagès rock shelters*

Prehistory is omnipresent around Tursac. The Ruth hamlet offers a visit to the Cellier shelter, with its engraved walls from 30,000 years ago. When it was excavated in 1927, a block of stone decorated with the head of an ibex was found, as well as stones engraved with vulva. One can also visit the Pagès (or Ruth) shelter, whose stratigraphy extends from the Aurignacian to the Magdalenian and which revealed a fine and plentiful lithic industry to its explorer D. Peyrony, in 1908.

Between Le Moustier and Tursac, the Facteur shelter (or Forêt shelter), which was peopled in the Aurignacian period and in the Gravettian, contained a female statuette: the Venus of Tursac. The beautiful Forêt cave, discovered in 1952, held clay models. Glory found engravings of animals, above all reindeer. The works date from the Magdalenian. One can also note other prehistoric deposits, at Liveyre, Roque-Barbel, Langle, Boulou (Aurignacian) etc. without running out of the names of the many sites in the region.

At Marzac, the Longue-Roche site, excavated by D. Peyrony, showed there had been an active lithic industry there, dating from the Middle and Upper Magdalenian, and the Azilian. As a result, L. Coulonges gave the name Longueroquian to the Perigordian Azilian period (9,000 B.C.).

***Préhistoparc***

Between Tursac and Les Eyzies, both children and adults will enjoy and profit from a visit to Préhistoparc where various prehistoric scenes are reproduced: a mammoth hunt, daily life, burial, a rhinoceros charging etc. This provides a pleasant and instructive walk through Périgord's history-filled countryside. The park was set up following the advice of Professor J. L. Heim, and makes it easier to understand the evolution and the life of our ancestors.

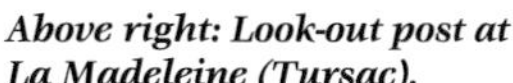

***Above right: Look-out post at La Madeleine (Tursac).***

***Right: Funeral rites. Tursac Préhistoparc.***

*Reconstitution of daily life. Tursac Préhistoparc.*

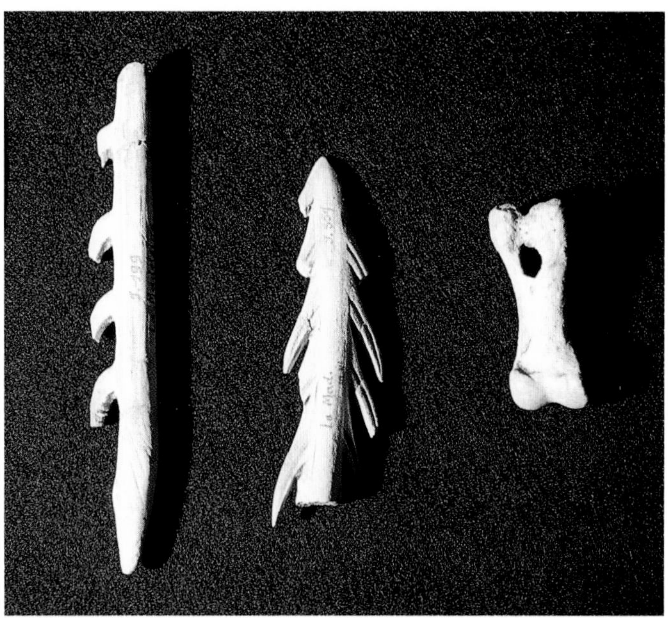

*Magdalenian harpoons and, right, a whistle.* **National Museum of Prehistory at Les Eyzies.**

*Needle with an eye, point and harpoon.* **National Museum of Prehistory at Les Eyzies.**

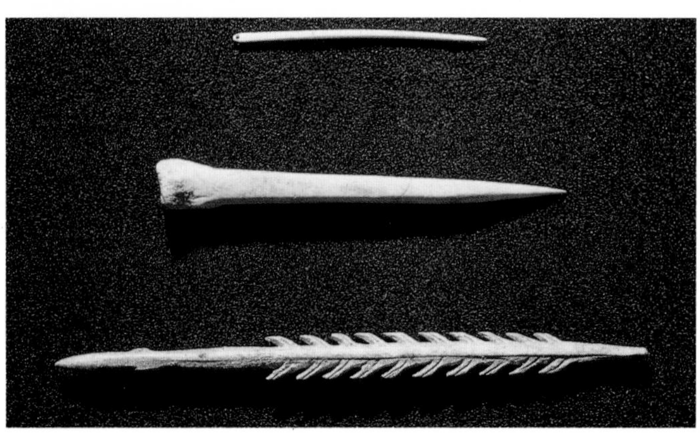

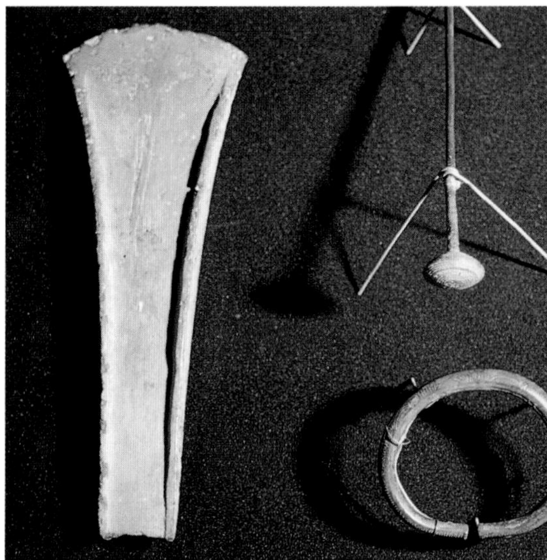

*Metal age: bronze axe, button pin, bracelet, tip of a pike.* **Pér**

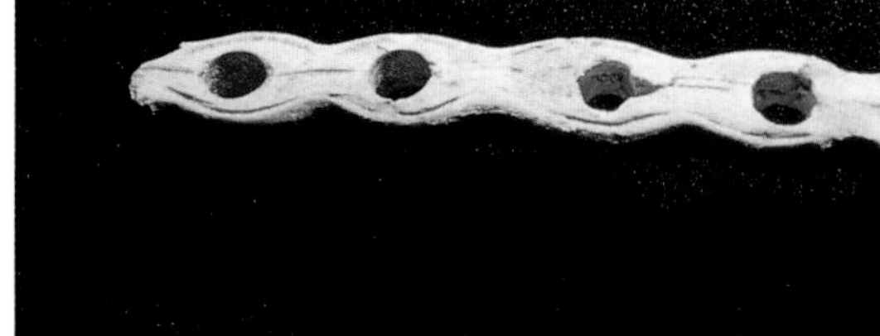

*Pierced baton.* **Périgord Museum, Périgueux.**

*Fishing scene.*
*Tursac Préhistoparc.*

*Magdalenian tomb at Saint-Germain-la-Rivière.*
**National Museum of Prehistory at Les Eyzies.**

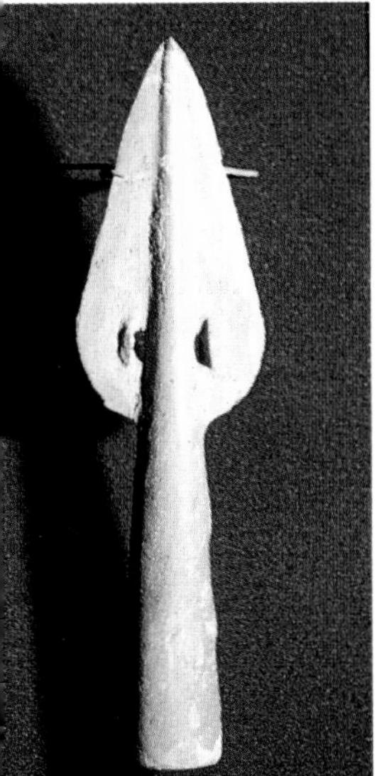

**eum, Périgueux.**

*Mammoth hunt. Tursac Préhistoparc.*

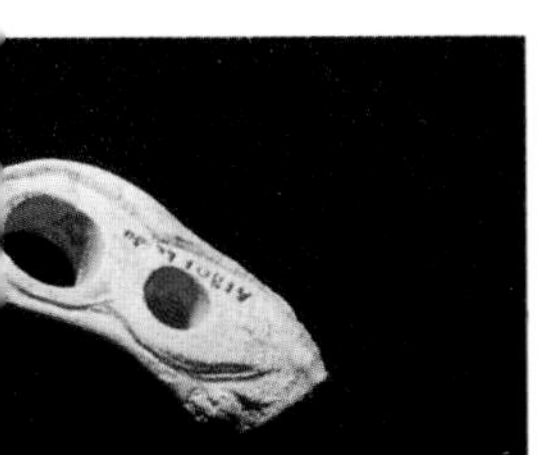

*Spear thrower.* **National Museum of Prehistory at Les Eyzies.**

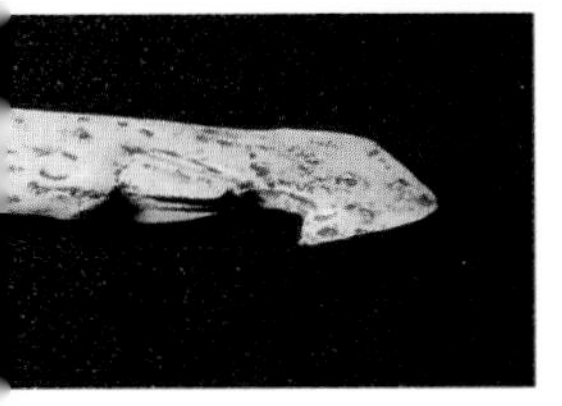

*The valley of the river Beune. On the hill, the little town of Sireuil.*

## Following the Beunes, from the Sarladais to Les Eyzies

Route 4

We shall leave the valley of the Vézère briefly, to cross Sarlat country and the springs of two trout rivers: the big and the small Beune. Although they are little known, the Beune valleys are very rich in prehistoric deposits, particularly in the communes of Meyrals and Marquay.

*Entrance to the Bernifal cave.*

### Bernifal and the little Beune

The road from Sarlat to Les Eyzies passes by several châteaux which each holds a shelter or a decorated cave, either in their own cellar or nearby.

When you visit the Puymartin château, you probably do not know that it overhangs an engraved cave. Further on, the Renaissance château of Beyssac dominates the Sarlat-Les Eyzies road. Beneath the château the Beyssac cave, inhabited during prehistoric times, reveals traces of paintings whose authenticity is under discussion. There are two neighbouring deposits of the same type; Beyssac II and the Moulin de Beyssac. Isolated on its rocky terrace, one finds the château du Roch. And not far away, the Roch prehistoric site and cave, discovered by Abbé Breuil, which holds an engraved horse, perhaps from the Gravettian period. One can also see the Roch Mousterian deposit and that of the Pas d'Estret, dating back from the Aurignacian and early Perigordian eras. The engraved Charretou cave, next door, is difficult to decipher.

The main site, open to the general public, is the Bernifal cave, not far from the left bank of the little Beune. It was discovered in 1902 by D. Peyrony, studied by

*High cave shelters dug out on the Sarlat-Les Eyzies road.*

Breuil and then by Leroi-Gourhan. It contains over one hundred figures, half painted and half engraved. There are many mammoths and tectiforms (signs in the shape of a roof, shelter or hut), as well as a famous engraved ass. Certain mammoths are almost the same as those of Rouffignac. They also date from the Upper Magdalenian period (12,000 B.C.). There are three other decorated caves on the same bank of the little river Beune. The entrance to the Bison cave is surrounded by other cavities, one of which is a cluzeau, or shelter dug into the cliff. It was excavated in 1957 by Abbé Glory, and revealed two hands painted in negative and engravings which are very difficult to date. The Sous-Grand-Lac cave, discovered in 1969 and studied by G. and B. Delluc and Leroi-Gourhan, contains a variety of engravings including a famous representation of a human figure, which can be compared with that of Saint-Cirq-du-Bugue and which may be contemporary with it. Lower down, La Calévie cave, discovered by Peyrony in 1903 and studied by Abbé Breuil, was inhabited both in the Magdalenian period and in the

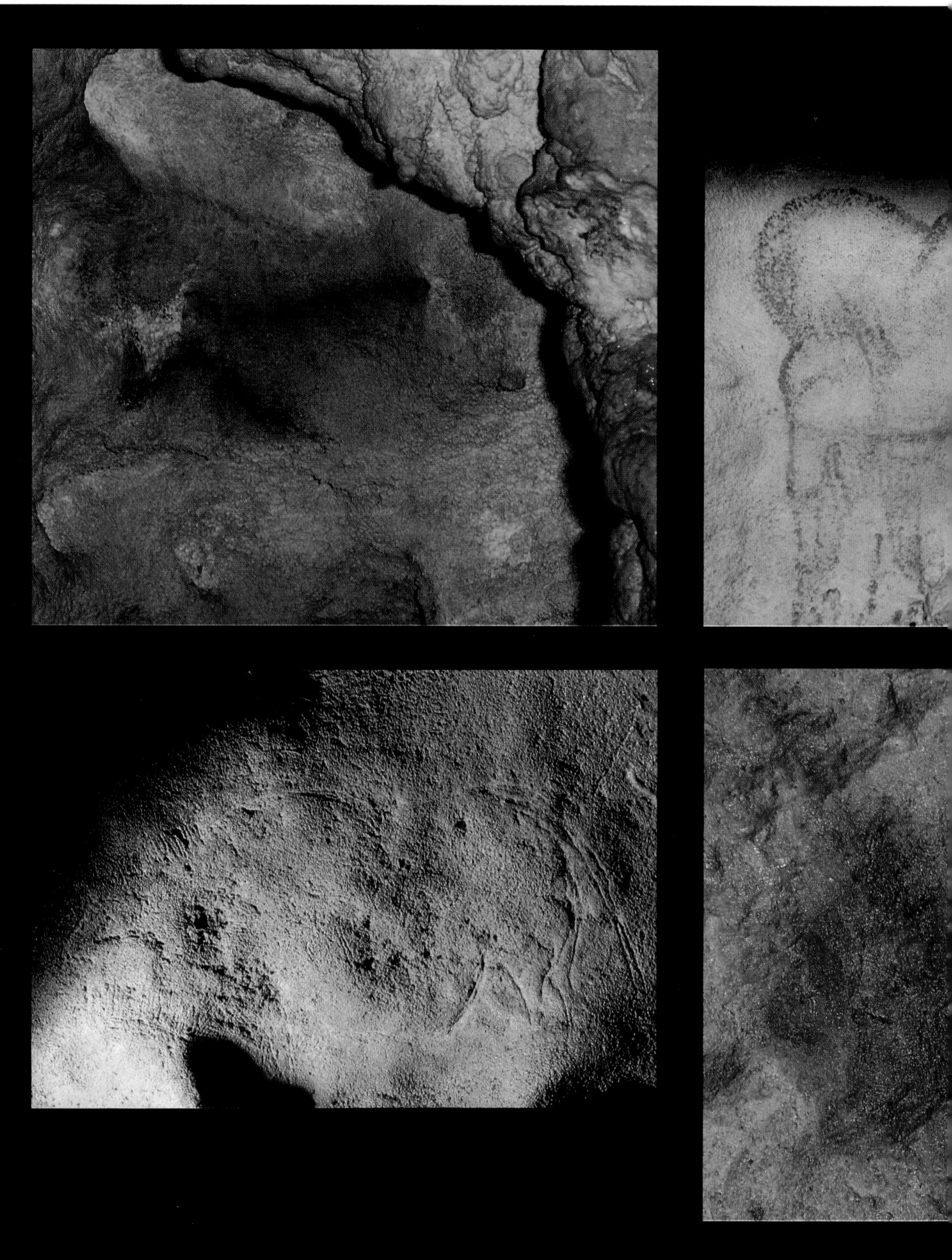

Bronze Age. Inside, they found mainly engravings of horses, dating from 15,000 B.C., and a bison modelled in clay. Four fine bronze bracelets, also discovered in the cave, can be seen in the Périgord museum, in Périgueux. Up-river, the Partisans' cave produced a tomb from the early Bronze Age (1,600 B.C.). The

***Bernifal cave.***
***Top left:***
***Ibex painted while grazing.***
Site photo.

***Top right:***
***mammoth painted in clay.***
Photo Aujoulat.

***High dug-out shelters and remains of troglodyte dwellings in Cazelle.***

Vielmouly II cave contains traces of engravings and paintings which have not yet been identified.

## Meyrals, the Rhonie Fort

Two kilometres (about one mile) from Bernifal, next to the Sarlat-Les Eyzies road, the Cazelle rock guards the remains of a troglodyte fort. A little further

***Bernifal cave.***
***Bottom left:***
***engraved bison.***
Photo Pémendant.

***Bottom right:***
***tectiform sign painted in iron oxide.***
Photo Aujoulat.

east, in the cliffs bordering the road, one can catch glimpses of *cluzeaux*, or cave shelters, high up.

To the east of Meyrals, the troglodyte fort of le Rhonie is open to visitors. It can be reached by a wooded path, bordered with bories, dry-stone huts. The fort was occupied at many times, dating from Prehistory to the Middle Ages.

## Marquay: Cap-Blanc and the big Beune

The little village of Marquay, perched on its hill between the two Beune rivers, holds many prehistoric sites: Masnègre, dating from the Perigordian period, Cacaro, Pageyral, le Pigeonnier and the Bout-du-Monde as well as La Grézélie, a cave with concretions.

Five kilometres (3 miles) further west, the Cap-Blanc shelter is unforgettable. It contains one of the most impressive prehistoric friezes known. There are deeply carved horse sculptures over a length of 13 metres (44 ft.) and a horned animal which seems to be jumping out of the wall. Their dimensions (the central horse in high relief is 2.2 metres long - 7 feet) and their artistic quality give the frieze an extraordinary impression of realism. These works probably date from the

***Part of the carved frieze. Cap-Blanc (Marquay).***
Photo J. Archambeau.

early or middle Magdalenian period (13,000 B.C.). Excavations carried out since 1909, sometimes with insufficient care, nonetheless revealed a sepulchre containing the remains of a person probably of the Cro-Magnon type, and various tools prove that the shelter was inhabited until the end of Magdalenian times. This major site, discovered in 1910 interested Peyrony, Breuil and all the leading prehistorians.

Very close to this, the La Grèze cave-shelter, open to the public, was decorated in Gravettian or Perigordian times. It contains a deep carving of a very old bison, from about 20,000 years ago, presented in profile with the horns full-face. Other animal engravings complete the decoration. This cave was discovered in 1904, and excavated by Breuil and Peyrony.

***Above and below: detail from the frieze of engraved horses. Cap-Blanc (Marquay).***

## Sireuil: Commarque and Laussel

The little village of Sireuil, high above the valleys of the two Beunes, tributaries of the Vézère, also has important prehistoric deposits (we are not far from Les Eyzies): Crabillat, Cazelle (Aurignacian and Mag-

***Commarque (Sireuil): below the castle, the troglodyte village and the prehistoric cave.***

dalenian), Barry, and above all the Nancy cave. This was discovered in 1913 and then studied by Abbé Breuil, and holds several animal engravings (horses, bison, ibex) drawn in the lower Magdalenian period (15,000 B.C.). Not far away, in 1900, a female statuette, 9 cm high, was discovered, called the "Venus of Sireuil". This beautiful figure, in ambered calcite, is displayed in the museum of Saint-Germain-en-Laye. Several other caves in the commune contain traces of paintings and engravings, which may not be from Palaeolithic times, even though most of these sites were occupied by prehistoric man: Font-Martine, Archambeau, Le Pilier, Le Rouillet.

Four kilometres (2.5 miles) east of Sireuil, difficult of access, and isolated from the hamlets around by a thick forest, overlooking a swampy vale irrigated by the Beune, Commarque seems to be a ghost château. It is a perfect example of a medieval Périgord fortress, but these days it is a vast ruin invaded until recently by trees and brambles. Its high keep dominates the remains of a village which previously was surrounded by gigantic ramparts. One can say that time stopped here. The site was inhabited in very ancient times, since beneath the castle one finds a prehistoric cave discovered by Breuil in 1915 and studied by most of the leading prehistorians, including A. Leroi-Gourhan. It revealed a sculpted horse, one of the most beautiful of prehistory, reminiscent of its "neighbours" from Cap-Blanc, and engravings of horses, ibex and female figures, dating from the Magdalenian period (12,000 B.C.). The cliff between the cave and the XIIIth century castle is dotted with a network of shelters, the remains of a troglodyte fort, probably carved out around the IXth or Xth century. This succession of habitats, a long line of history of humanity, frozen in time, a time which ended 500 years ago, is both impressive and worrying.

Above the Beune swamps, opposite the formidable Commarque fortress, the Laussel castle dating from the XVth and XVIth century, even though it has been fully restored, still preserves its elegant silhouette and its machicolated towers. Near the castle one can see a curious troglodyte pigeon house and the famous Laussel prehistoric site, which has revealed one of the most important stratigraphic sequences of the Middle and Upper Palaeolithic. It is on ten levels spanning the lower Mousterian (100,000 B.C.) to the upper Solutrean (17,000 B.C.). Between these two extremes, the specialists found typical Mousterian remains (70,000 B.C.), Châtelperronian (35,000 B.C.), Aurignacian (30,000 B.C.) and finally Gravettian, upper Périgordian and lower Solutrean (25,000 to 20,000 B.C.). At the latter level, five low-reliefs representing human beings were found: a man, the "hunter", who seems to be throwing a spear and four women with breasts and heavy hips, including the famous "Venus of Laussel" sculpted in a golden-coloured stone. This old lady, 42 centimetres high (16.5 inches), holds a bison's horn and is among the most famous female representations from Prehistory. She can be seen either in the Bordeaux museum or in the Les Eyzies museum where there is a mould. The different shelters making up the site, excavated by La Rivière in 1894 and then by Lalanne in 1908, have also produced a great variety of tools from different epochs.

The confluence of the Beunes and the Vézère leads us directly to the ancient and modern capital of Prehistory: Les Eyzies.

***Dug-out cave shelters at Commarque.***

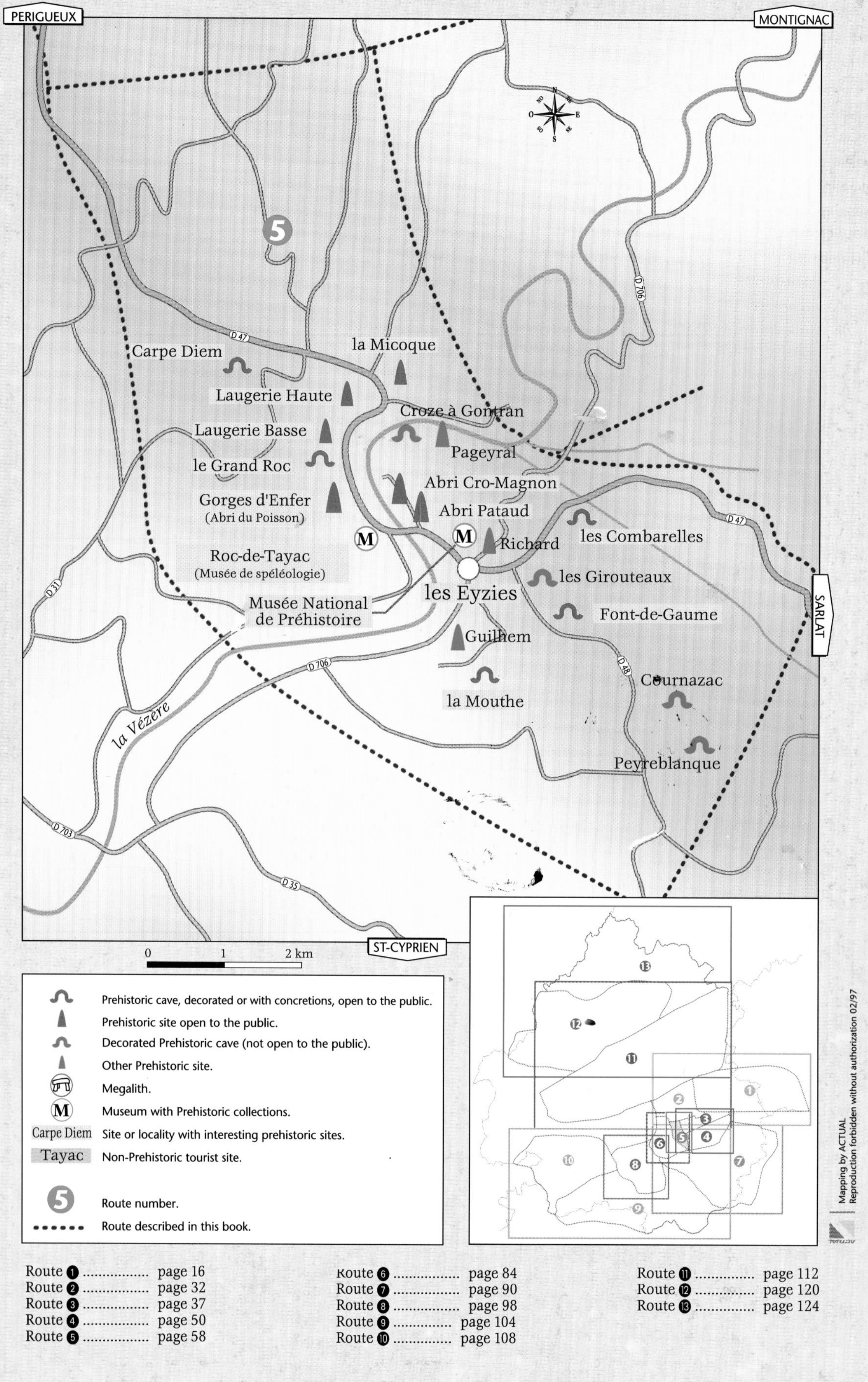
PERIGUEUX
MONTIGNAC
SARLAT
ST-CYPRIEN
N
E
S
O
NO
NE
SO
SE
5
D 47
D 706
D 31
D 703
D 35
D 48
Carpe Diem
la Micoque
Laugerie Haute
Laugerie Basse
Croze à Gontran
Pageyral
le Grand Roc
Abri Cro-Magnon
Gorges d'Enfer
(Abri du Poisson)
Abri Pataud
M
Richard
les Combarelles
Roc-de-Tayac
(Musée de spéléologie)
les Girouteaux
les Eyzies
Musée National
de Préhistoire
Font-de-Gaume
Guilhem
Cournazac
la Mouthe
la Vézère
Peyreblanque
0
1
2 km
Prehistoric cave, decorated or with concretions, open to the public.
Prehistoric site open to the public.
Decorated Prehistoric cave (not open to the public).
Other Prehistoric site.
Megalith.
Museum with Prehistoric collections.
Carpe Diem
Site or locality with interesting prehistoric sites.
Tayac
Non-Prehistoric tourist site.
Route number.
Route described in this book.
13
12
11
1
2
3
4
5
6
7
8
9
10

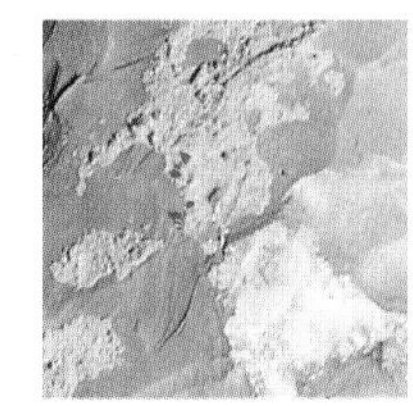

# Les Eyzies, travelling back in time

***Les Eyzies: Cro-Magnon shelter.***

## *Sites open to visitors at Les Eyzies*

*National Museum of Prehistory, tel. 05.53.06.97.03.*
***Font-de-Gaume** cave, tel. 05.53.06.90.80.*
***Combarelles** cave, tel. 05.53.06.97.22. or 05.53.06.90.80.*
***La Mouthe** cave: temporarily closed.*

***La Micoque** prehistoric site*
***Laugerie-Haute** shelter*
***Poisson** shelter*
***Gorge d'Enfer** vale*
***Lartet** shelter*
***Oreille d'Enfer** shelter*
*tel. 05.53.06.90.80.*

***Pataud** shelter and on-site museum, tel. 05.53.06.92.46.*
***Cro-Magnon** shelter: visible near the hotel.*

***Laugerie-Basse** shelter and museum*
***Grand-Roc** cave with concretions*
*tel. 05.53.06.92.70.*

***Carpe-Diem** cave with concretions,*
*tel. 05.53.06.91.07.*
*Roc de Tayac fort and museum of Speleology,*
*tel. 05.53.35.43.77.*

***Les Eyzies** Tourist Office: tel. 05.53.06.97.05.*

*The GR 6 and 36 meet at Les Eyzies and enable one to discover sites and cliffs. One can also visit the garden of medicinal plants.*

# Les Eyzies, the worldwide Prehistoric Capital

Route 5

## Site and history

It is normal to present Les Eyzies as the World capital of Prehistory. The many decorated caves and, particularly the rock shelters, can only confirm this idea. The many styles and epochs, not only from Prehistory but also from Historic times, make Les Eyzies a time capsule. This vast "stationary visit" can make us appreciate prehistoric times better, from the Micoquian to Laugerie-Basse (from 450,000 to 5,000 B.C.). The prehistory of Les Eyzies, has lasted a hundred times longer than History, and two hundred times longer than the Christian era.

Even if Prehistory was not present at every stage, Les Eyzies is worth a visit, even if only for the site. At the confluence of the Vézère and the Beune, the little village, with its castle transformed into a museum, clings under the high cliffs carved out with rock shelters, pierced with caves and troglodyte dwellings, crowned with oaks and junipers. After crossing the Vézère, one finds a little road which winds between river and rock: the "royal way" of Prehistory, an unimaginable succes-

*View of Les Eyzies, world capital of Prehistory.*

sion of caves and shelters, in impressive surroundings of cliffs.

To begin with, Les Eyzies was no more than a hamlet belonging to Tayac. The population was probably fairly large in the VIIIth to IXth century, proved by the numerous troglodyte dwellings and fortified hamlets to resist the attacks of the Vikings. These can be seen on the site of the museum, at the entrance to Les Eyzies, at the Roc de Tayac, the Laugerie-Basse, the Cazelles rock, Girouteaux, near Font-de-Gaume and at the Guilhem troglodyte chapel. The cliffs are pitted with *cluzeaux* or "look-out posts", artificial caves pierced high up in

***The National Museum of Prehistory, above the little town of Les Eyzies.***

***The cliff overlooking the river Vézère at Les Eyzies-de-Tayac.***

**Remains of semi-troglodyte structures in Les Eyzies, leaving the village towards Sarlat.**

## The enigma of the prehistoric population

*One cannot estimate the population of Les Eyzies, even though its importance in prehistoric times cannot be contested. Certain researchers prefer the idea of a very small social unit, so that the hunters did not use up their territory too quickly. But one can also think, because of the outstanding artistic artefacts, that such a culture could only be born from a numerous and structured population. The deep layer of carved flints, found on certain sites, is not conclusive either. This could also be the result of a very large population working for years, or a small group working for centuries. But the structures within the layers favour the theory of a dense population.*

the rock, and which make one wonder how the occupants could reach them. One can also find very fine Bories, dry-stone huts and difficult to date, in Le Télégraphe and La Rouquette. In the Xth or XIth centuries, the lords of Tayac built a strong fortress set in the rock, which passed to the Beynacs in 1322. Tayac still remained the major site, with its monastery built in the XIIth century, whose fortified church still remains. Built on an overhanging rock, the troglodyte fort of the Roc de Tayac was another fortress used as a toll post controlling the river. Occupied by the English troops, the fort was besieged by the lord of Beynac in 1381. The English of Tayac conquered the Sarladais region in 1408 but the French retook it in 1411. During the Wars of Religion, the Beynacs became Protestant. Jean-Guy de Beynac-Tayac, who remained Catholic, and held the Les Eyzies castle, laid siege to Saint Cyprien in 1590. After plotting against Henri IV in 1605, in revenge against the beheading of his friend Biron, he was condemned to death, and then pardoned by Turenne. The castle was abandoned in the XVIIIth century. In a state of ruin and destruction, it was bought by the State in 1913 and transformed into the National Museum of Prehistory.

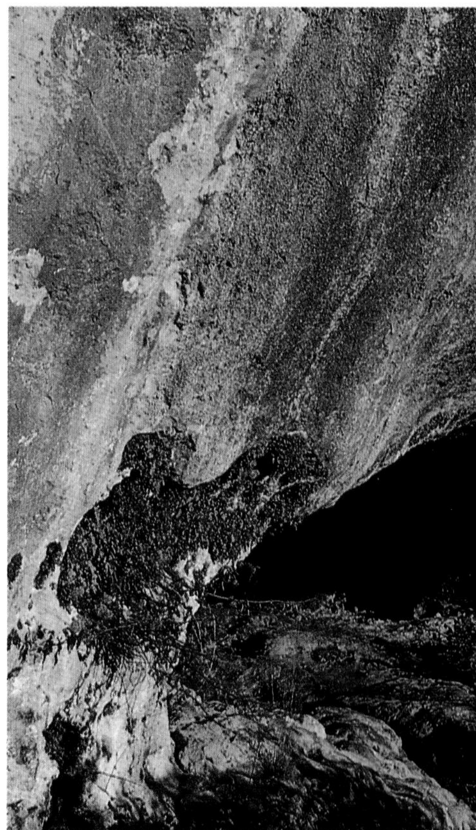

## The Birth of Prehistory

Prehistory is a young science: barely a century old. The first real "excavation" took place in 1862, in the Richard cave in Les Eyzies. In 1863, Edouard Lartet (1801-1871), father of human Palaeontology, teamed with the Englishman Henry Christy to excavate at La Madeleine (Tursac) and at Laugerie-Haute.

In 1868, when the Périgueux-Agen railway was built, five skeletons were found in the Cro-Magnon rock shelter. The link between prehistoric man and modern man had been found. The prehistorians understood that they had discovered a fantastic treasure, and never left Les Eyzies after that. Interest grew when the first decorated caves were found: La Mouthe in 1895, and Font-de Gaume and les Combarelles in 1901. These first prehistorians, fully aware that they were writing a new page of human knowledge, included scholars, keen amateurs, teachers, many priests, because Prehistory brought a revolution to their concept of the world, as well as many local farmers who knew the land and lived with Prehistory on a daily basis. Among them, three figures stand out: Breuil, Peyrony and Capitan, three men who worked together.

But even before these three prehistorians, an adopted son of Périgord should be mentio-

*Rock shelter, Les Eyzies.*

*A fire burns in a shelter at Les Eyzies, warming both the body and the heart of Man.*

*Above the castle shelter,*
***D. and E. Peyrony bronze plates,***
***among the remains of***
***troglodyte structures.***

## The fathers of Prehistory

• *Abbé Breuil (1877-1961) came to Périgord in 1897. He was a great analyst of cave wall art, and was the first to set down a chronology of Prehistory (subdivisions of the Upper Palaeolithic, 1911). In 1929 the first chair of Prehistory was created for him at the Collège de France. He travelled throughout the world looking for traces of the first men, working in particular with Teilhard de Chardin. He was nicknamed «the pope of Prehistory».*

• *Denis Peyrony (1869-1954) was born and died in Dordogne. He was a teacher at Les Eyziës, and the first great discoverer of caves, a tireless excavator and a stratigrapher of genius. He created the museum at Les Eyzies and was its first curator (1918). He defined the existence of the Perigordian culture, parallel to the Aurignacian.*

• *Capitan (1854-1929), a doctor, also led many excavations. He was named professor at the Collège de France in 1907.*

ned; Jouannet, whose discoveries right at the beginning of the XIXth century could not shake the "biblical certitudes" of the scholars of his time. The seriousness of his approach to his work merits giving him the title "grandfather of Prehistory".

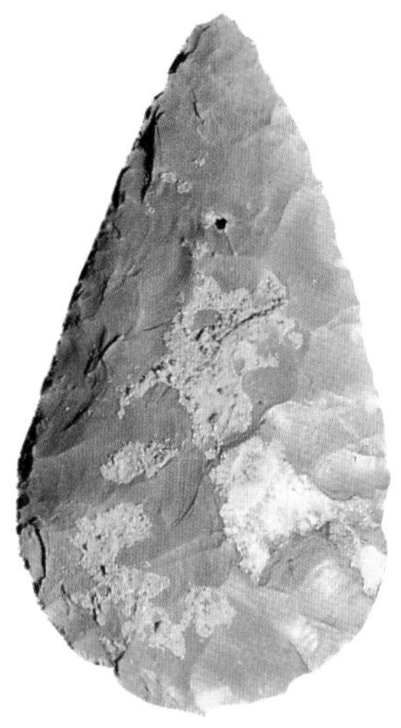

***Biface from the early Palaeolithic, about 300,000 years old.*** **National Museum of Prehistory at Les Eyzies.**

Nowadays, excavations are still continuing in Les Eyzies, perhaps even more intensely than ever. After all, the earth is a gigantic book which still needs its pages turning and has in no way given up all its secrets. The prehistorians are perfectly aware of this, and most of them have a country residence in the commune.

## The National Museum of Prehistory

The Les Eyzies castle, bought by the State in 1913, encouraged by Peyrony, is itself built on a prehistoric site and a troglodyte village. The castle cave, from the Magdalenian era, contained a famous bone engraved with nine persons marching past a bison. The edifice became the museum of Prehistory in 1923. Today, it holds several millions of objects. The clear method of presentation and the very complete range of treasures make it an easy and fascinating museum for visitors. Moreover, it is the leading prehistoric museum in France for its number of visitors, and the second in the world, after Saint-Germain-en-Laye, for the wealth of its collections. Following the initiative of Jean Guichard, its curator, and his successor, J.-J. Cleyet-Merle, a highly developed project should see the surface area quadrupled.

The visit we describe corresponds to the former layout of the museum. The structure will be greatly transformed when works have ended.

The visit begins on the third floor of the keep, with the lithic industries room, the "country of chipped stones", presented chronologically. From the worked pebbles of Australopithecus three million years ago, the Abbevillian and Clactonian industries follow (500,000 B.C.), and then the Acheulian (400,000 to 120,000 B.C.) of Homo erectus. Then, in the Mousterian, under the "reign" of Neanderthal man, scrapers became more numerous. The Aurignacian and its parallel culture, the Perigordian, (35,000 to 20,000 B.C.) saw the appearance of the bone industry and art (jewellery). The Solutrean is known for its "laurel leaf" carved stones, real works of art, and for its needles with eyes. The Magdalenian (15,000 to 9,000 B.C.) saw the discovery of harpoons and fish-hooks. The Azilian, Epipalaeolithic and, at the end of the Palaeolithic, the Sauveterrian and the Tardenoisian, typified by microliths, are also on show, as well as several specimens from the Neolithic and the Bronze Age. Window displays demonstrate the development of the main objects: the biface, the all-purpose tool for 600,000 years, the scraper, the burin and the point.

*Laboratory of the National Museum of Prehistory, built by Froidevaux in 1963-1966.*

The second floor of the keep is mainly devoted to art and the bone industry. A first room presents various engraved blocks of stone from between 35,000 and 9,000 B.C., coming from sites in the region: La Ferrassie, Sergeac, Les Eyzies, La Madeleine. Essentially, these are female symbols, as on the famous Lalinde Rock, and animals such as the aurochs from the Fourneau du Diable. The second room

***Engraved vulva, beginning of the Upper Palaeolithic, Aurignacian.***
**National Museum of Prehistory at Les Eyzies.**

shows portable art, decorated sticks and spear-throwers, weapons, domestic objects (needles, awls, whistles), ornaments (necklaces and pendants in bone, deer teeth, shells and fossils), female statuettes (copies of the Venus of Sireuil, the Venus of Tursac and the famous Venus of Brassempouy), and phallic motifs.

On the first floor, the room with mouldings and iconographical documents contains maps, chronological tables and explanations. The Breuil room displays the most recent acquisitions of the museum. On the ground floor the "sepulchral" and "prehistoric fauna" rooms of the Renaissance building contain a summary of the first discoveries, the methods of excavation, and the descriptions of certain sites. One display contains a series of skulls: Neanderthal man, Cro-Magnon man etc. The tombs of Roc du Barbeau (Sauveterrian) and of Saint-Germain-la-Rivière (Magdalenian) are reconstituted. A final room is dedicated to specimens of fauna (aurochs, reindeer, bears).

Before leaving the museum, take advantage of the splendid panorama from the terrace, and do not forget to salute the stone guardian of the museum, *primitive man*, without committing the usual error of mixing him up with "Cro-

***1 - Points of different origins and ages, for spears, throwers and arrows.*** **National Museum of Prehistory at Les Eyzies.**

***2 - Worked shingle stone, the first tool of the first man.*** **National Museum of Prehistory at Les Eyzies.**

***3 - Chopper: primitive stone tool. The most rudimentary expression of the lithic industry.*** **National Museum of Prehistory at Les Eyzies.**

***4 - Bifaces: almond, oval or triangular shaped, these "all-purpose tools" from Prehistory are from 4 1/2 to 6 1/2 inches long.*** **National Museum of Prehistory at Les Eyzies.**

***5 - Composite variegated tools, chisel, awl etc.:*** **National Museum of Prehistory at Les Eyzies.**

3

5

*Carved phalli, all found in Périgord.* **National Museum of Prehistory at Les Eyzies.**

*Anthropomorphic shapes engraved on bone, upper Magdalenian, about 10,000 B.C.* **National Museum of Prehistory at Les Eyzies.**

Magnon". He could be insulted! In fact, working from Neanderthal bones found at La Chapelle-aux-Saints (Corrèze), the sculptor Paul Dardé created this primitive man in 1930, whose intelligence awakens while contemplating the splendid decor of the valley.

## Decorated caves Font-de-Gaume, the magic art of polychromy

Leaving Les Eyzies, on the Sarlat road, a steep path alongside the cliff and then a narrow, twisted entrance, which seems made to illustrate a Jules Verne novel or a film by Walt Disney, leads to Font-de-Gaume. The cave, which is open to the public, offers a fine collection of engravings and polychrome paintings, most dating back to the Magdalenian epoch (12,000 B.C.). Carved flints (burins, scrapers and blades) and other objects found during the excavations, together with numerous graffiti which, unfortunately spoil some of the paintings, are evidence that the cave was frequented almost continuously from Mousterian times until our days. It was discovered in 1901 by D. Peyrony,

*Carved horse, Mould at the* **National Museum of Prehistory at Les Eyzies.**

and the 130 metre (140 yds) long passage holds about 250 drawings authenticated by Capitan and Abbé Breuil, who catalogued them. The visitor can see about thirty of the most beautiful and best preserved. Everything possible has been done to conserve these treasures: the walls have been cleaned, sprayed with formolized water to avoid the spread of micro-organisms, the lighting is low and at ground level.

After walking 60 metres (65 yds) underground, one comes to a bottle-neck, called the Rubicon, which marks the beginning of the decorated part. Red points on the wall herald it. A series of stick patterns also marks the end of the gallery. These signs are found in many caves, but what is their significance? A sanctuary, as A. Leroi-Gourhan thinks? This seems probable. One thing is certain, the caves were never used as living quarters. Excavations have revealed no signs of permanent occupation.

After "crossing" the Rubicon, the first frieze comes into view: a dozen mammoths and bison. Engravings and pain-

***The Font-de-Gaume cliff at Les Eyzies.***

tings are associated. Finely engraved contours accompany the black outline. The paint was then applied to the limestone wall. Two colours predominate: red and black. Here again, as at Lascaux, the relief of the rock itself is used to suggest volume. Further in, by the sition thus appears to be more peaceful. On the right, in a lateral passage, one discovers several bison, reindeer and horses, but somewhat damaged by calcite. Coming back to the main gallery, a huge frieze of five bison engraved and painted stands out from a white calcite

*Entrance to the Font-de-Gaume cave at Les Eyzies.*

intersection, on the left, one discovers the famous scene of confronting reindeer. A huge male towers over a female, hoofs upturned. Abbé Breuil saw this as a fight. However, one can see the tongue of the black reindeer licking the forehead of the female. The compo-

background. These paintings were rediscovered in 1966, once the clay-limestone gangue had been removed from the cave wall. On the right, a stratigraphic section shows the different levels of formation and occupation of the ground. At the end of the gallery, in a recess called the "bison chapel" one finds four polychrome bison amongst about twelve drawings. A more detailed visit reveals many other treasures: negative hands, tectiform signs, representations of humans. Even if the queue is long at the bottom of the cliff, be patient. Font-de-Gaume is worth it.

Nine hundred metres (980 yds) south, the Cournazac cave, discovered in 1976, holds a painting of a mammoth, engravings and lines drawn by fingers. Further south again, the Peyreblanque cave contains traces of paintings. To the north, the Girouteaux cave contains non-identified engravings.

## Les Combarelles, the horse paradise

The Combarelles cave, discovered in 1901, studied by Capitan, Breuil and Peyrony, and also open to visitors, can be found near the Sarlat road, 1.5 kilometres (1 mile) from Font-de-Gaume. There are about 800 wall engravings spread along 300 metres (330 yds) of this winding underground passage. There is a real profusion of intermingled engravings over the last 120 metres (130 yds) of walls: mammoths, ibex, kiang, bears, reindeer, deer, woolly rhinoceros, bison, horses. The horse is the animal most frequently represented: there are nearly 140 horses. These engravings date from the Middle and Upper Magdalenian period (12,000 to 10,000 B.C.). The cave is also famous for its 48 representations of human beings. Among the masks,

***Two examples from the big polychrome bison frieze. Font-de-Gaume (Les Eyzies).***
Photo H. Champollion.

***Calcite covered the cave-wall and protected this painted horse. Font-de-Gaume (Les Eyzies).***
***Reindeer and bison at the turning between the main galleryand the axial gallery. Font-de-Gaume (Les Eyzies)***
Photos H. Champollion.

hands and various silhouettes, one can make out a seated person, presented in profile, with members out of proportion. This makes one wonder why human representations are so rare and so unrealistic. The debate is still open. Among the other curiosities of this cave, one must admire the engraving of a lioness, a kiang, an ibex, one of the rare paintings in Combarelles and, above all, that of a reindeer bending down to drink. The engravings are often incomplete, and

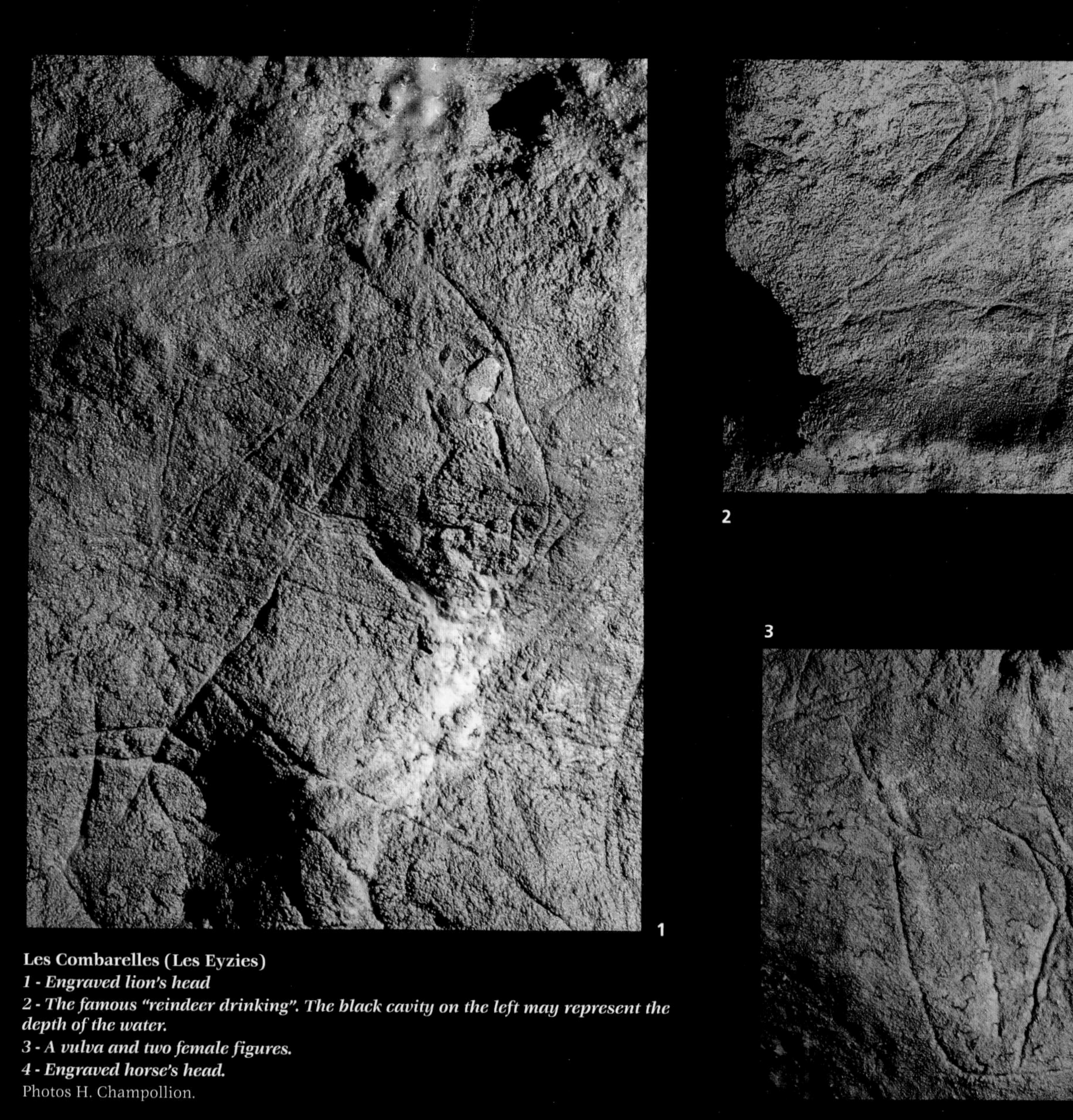


**Les Combarelles (Les Eyzies)**
***1 - Engraved lion's head***
***2 - The famous "reindeer drinking". The black cavity on the left may represent the depth of the water.***
***3 - A vulva and two female figures.***
***4 - Engraved horse's head.***
Photos H. Champollion.

amongst the latticework of lines and signs the visitor can let his imagination run free, depending on the lighting angles.

The Combarelles II cave also holds about thirty engravings. Its entrance was excavated by Rivière as early as 1892. At the entry to the vale of Combarelles, the Rey cave has rendered Mousterian, Solutrean and Magdalenian tools. Abbé Breuil saw indecipherable and doubtful engravings there.

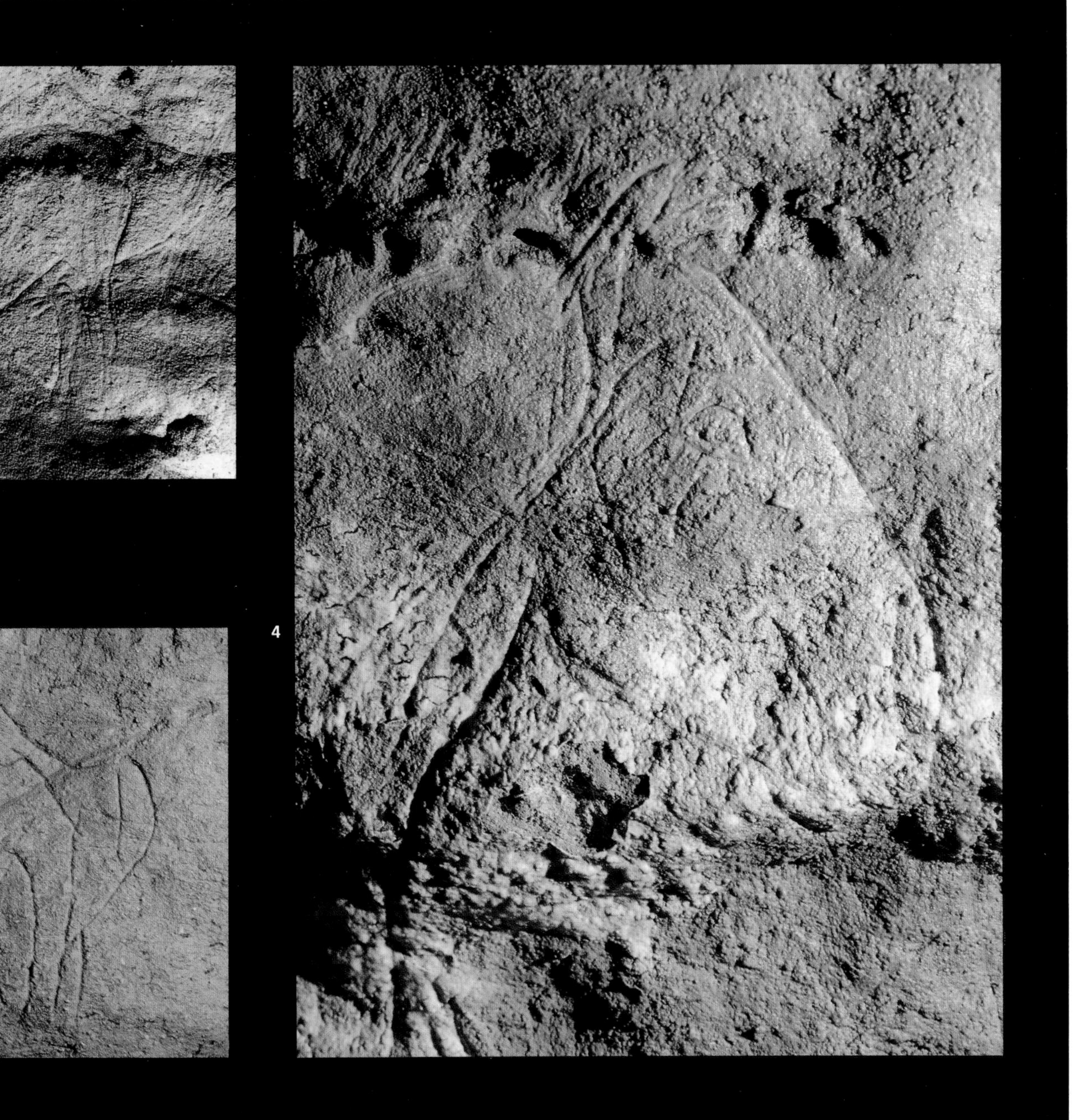

4

## La Mouthe, the first decorated cave discovered in Périgord

Two kilometres (about one mile) south of Les Eyzies, in the direction of La Mouthe cave, the road passes under the Roc de la Peine rocks, an overhanging platform which one can reach on foot, and which gives a wonderful panorama over the village. Le Mouthe cave, discovered in 1895, has been closed to the public since 1981 to avoid deterioration. It will not be opened up again until the works it contains, engravings enhanced by ochre lines, are no longer at risk. These works date from the Gravettian culture (25,000 B.C.) to the Upper Magdalenian (10,000 B.C.). After walking a hundred metres (110 yds), one comes to the first hall whose ceilings and left wall are decorated with deep engravings: a horse and four big horned cattle whose heads are out of proportion and are of archaic workmanship. The further one penetrates into the cave the more sophisticated the outline of the engraving becomes: bison, rhinoceros, ibex, mammoths, bulls, reindeer. Nonetheless, the principal curiosity is the representation of what is thought to be an engraved and painted prehistoric hut.

Around the cave there are several prehistoric sites: the Queylou cave, the Combe-

*Entrance to the La Mouthe cave.*

Bétou cave and the Gaubert shelter.

At Tayac, near the church, is the Croze à Gontran cave, named after an assassin who took refuge there last century. It was cleared in 1907 and holds several engravings which are difficult to make out. In the ceiling, there is a fine engraving of a huge horse. At the entrance and at the far end, one finds the usual series of enigmatic signs. Judging from their archaic aspect, Abbé Breuil dated these engravings back to the Aurignacian epoch (30,000 B.C.). Around the cave, the Crolus, Delluc, Demelle and Fournier rock shelters contain engravings which are difficult to identify and of doubtful origin.

## Shelters and sites

***La Micoque: at the dawn of humanity***

Here we present the main shelters where the populations of Les Eyzies lived, in chronological order of occupation, which appears to have been continuous.

The site of La Micoque has not only given its name to the Micoquian Age, its industrial facies is contemporary with the beginning of the Mousterian (100,000 B.C.). Its lowest level contained several flints which were clearly older, dating back to 450,000 B.C., chipped by the first inhabitants of Les Eyzies. It was occupied successively by Archanthropian man, whose best-known representative is Pithecanthropian man, and probably by the first *Homo sapiens:* Neanderthal man. La Micoque, excavated in 1895, allowed Peyrony to define the Micoquian and Tayacian Ages, the latter name being abandoned by certain prehistorians. Further excavations, starting in 1906, continued with Peyrony, Bordes and J.-Ph. Rigaud. The site is open to visitors.

*Excavations at La Micoque (Les Eyzies)*

*Excavations of the prehistoric site of La Micoque, at Les Eyzies, led by Jean-Philippe Rigaud and André Debenath.*

## *Aurignacian, Perigordian, Solutrean*

*Modern man, or Cro-Magnon man (in other words: ourselves), appeared around 32,000 B.C. He invented art, and decorated the first caves with drawings and engravings which were still primitive. The first civilization, called Aurignacian, defined by Abbé Breuil from the Aurignac cave in Haute Garonne, lasted from 32,000 to 25,000 B.C. In Périgord, it is characteristic of certain sites in Les Eyzies (Cro-Magnon, Pataud, Croze à Gontran) or in Castelmerle (Castenet and Blanchard shelters). From 25,000 to 17,000 B.C., the following period is named Gravettian. Tools and works of art diversified. Because of the importance of the Perigordian sites during these periods, in 1933 D. Peyrony superposed the description Perigordian on the Aurignacian and Gravettian, divided into 7 phases. Prehistorians still have different opinions on the question of this division. In Les Eyzies, the Gorge d'Enfer vale, the Pataud shelter, and those of Laugerie-Haute and Laussel are examples of Perigordian. From 18,000 to 16,000 B.C., the Solutrean period (named after Solutré in Saône-et-Loire) saw Man's taste for works of art develop. Flints were flaked into remarkable "laurel-leaf" points. Laugerie-Haute displays the complete stratigraphy of this epoch.*

1

2

3

4

### *Cro-Magnon, modern man*

The Audi shelter confirms occupation by Neanderthal man, its first level containing deposits from early Mousterian times (100,000 B.C.) and its second, from recent Mousterian (40,000 B.C.), just like the Chadourne shelter. Near the Pataud shelter, the Vignaud shelter also marks the transition to modern man. It contained one of the oldest paintings in the world: a stag's head.

But it was during the Aurignacian period (30,000 B.C.), with the "arrival" of *Homo sapiens sapiens,* that Les Eyzies and its surroundings saw a real demographic explosion and became the centre of the prehistoric world. Aurignacian man, who chose Périgord to live in and to create the first works of art, is known to us under the name of Cro-Magnon man. In the Cro-Magnon shelter, which can be seen near the hotel of the same name, five skeletons surrounded by jewellery and shells were discovered in 1868. They were studied by Lartet, who was able to define a human type tall in height (1.8 metres, about 6 feet) and very similar to us both concerning his physique and his cranial capacity. Did he come from Asia, as is said, or did he develop by mutation from preceding populations? It is difficult to know.

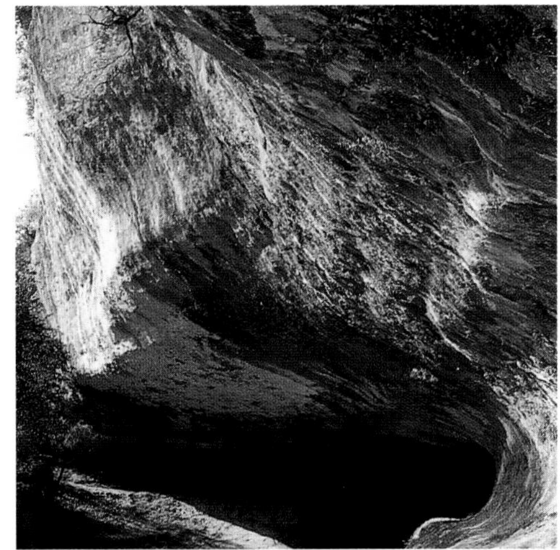

***The great shelter of the Gorge d'Enfer.***

### *Gorge d'Enfer and the Poisson shelter*

The vale of the Gorge d'Enfer, (Hell Gorge), which can be visited, includes seven prehistoric sites one of them a gigantic rock shelter. The Lartet and Pasquet shelters present characteristics typical of the Aurignacian period. The Lartet shelter, excavated by E. Lartet in 1868, revealed several pointed tips from the Châtelperronian period (35,000 B.C.) and fragments of painted stones, traces of ancient decoration by Auri-

***Opposite page:***
***1 - Stratigraphy of Laugerie-Haute west.***

***2 - Discovered at Laugerie-Haute, this engraved horned animal dates from the early Magdalenian period. National Museum of Prehistory at Les Eyzies.***

***3 - Laugerie-Haute (Les Eyzies).***

***4 - View of Laugerie-Haute west.***

***The Pasquet shelter, Gorge d'Enfer.***

visited by contacting the guide at Laugerie-Haute. To the south-west of the vale, the Abzac cave was occupied in the Magdalenian period.

***Herbivores engraved on a stone slab from the Oreille d'Enfer. Later Perigordian, about 25,000 years old.***
**National Museum of Prehistory at Les Eyzies.**

gnacian artists. The Pasquet shelter is representative of the end of the Aurignacian period.

Still in the Val d'Enfer, the Poisson (fish) shelter contains a first Aurignacian level, but the sculpture of an enormous salmon in the ceiling dates back to the Gravettian (25,000 B.C.) or Upper Perigordian (30,000 B.C.). This unusual situation explains why, although the cave was found in 1892, the fish itself was not discovered until 1912. Nearby, the Oreille d'Enfer shelter and cave date back to the same epoch and a block of stone from there, engraved with animals, can be seen in the museum of Les Eyzies. The Poisson and Oreille d'Enfer can be

### *The Pataud shelter, a remarkable on-site museum*

Discovered at the end of the XIXth century, the Pataud shelter was studied mainly by the American Movius. The fourteen archeological levels of the Pataud shelter cover the Aurignacian, Gravettian and early Solutrean periods (32,000 to 18,000 B.C.). A skull of the Cro-Magnon type, 20,000 years old, gave information about the end of the Perigordian. The shelter also contained a female figure. A superb ibex is engraved in the wall. Following the idea of Henry de Lumley, an on-site museum was opened in 1990. The public can discover sections through the deposits, and items found: tools, the skeleton of a young woman and her child, as well as a reconstitution of "Madame

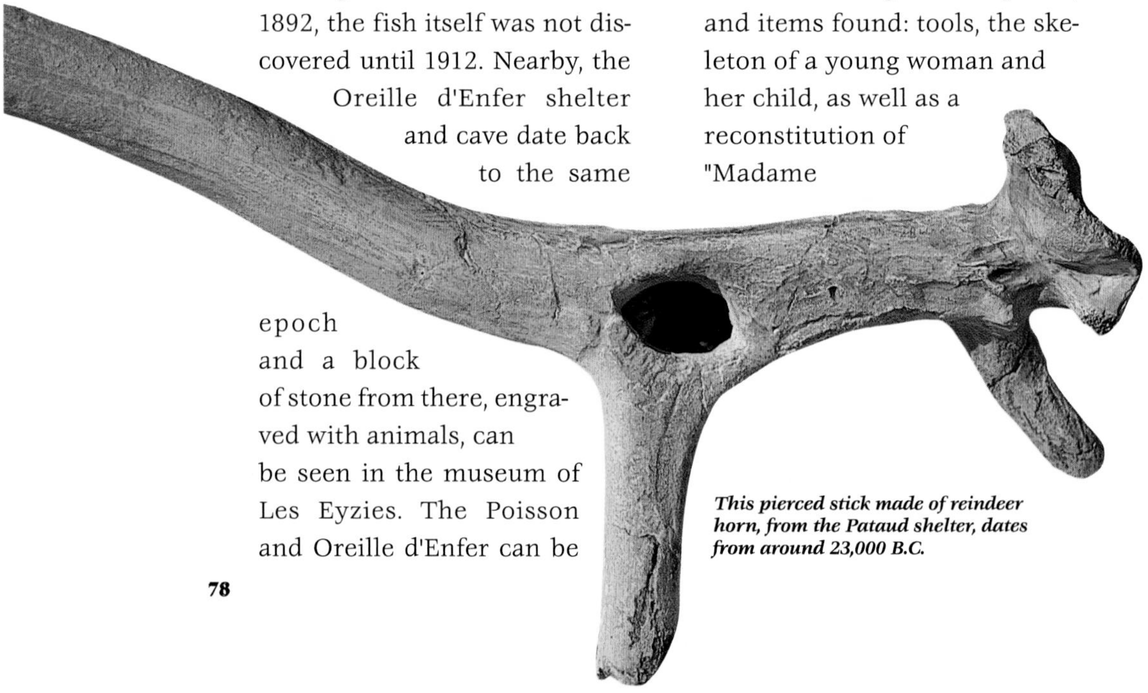

***This pierced stick made of reindeer horn, from the Pataud shelter, dates from around 23,000 B.C.***

*Mould of "Madame Pataud's" skull, about 21,000 B.C.*
**Museum of the Pataud shelter site.**

Pataud". The work of the prehistorian is presented under various forms: excavations, laboratory research etc. Finally, electronics, audiovisual aids and games provide a new and interesting approach to Prehistory.

***Laugerie-Haute, the standard for prehistoric chronology***

The vast Laugerie-Haute shelter, nearly 200 metres (220 yds) long and open to visitors, has been taken as the standard for establishing prehisto-

*Discovered at Laugerie-Haute, this bone engraving (mammoth hooves and trunks) dates from around 14,000 B.C.*
**National Museum of Prehistory at Les Eyzies.**

*Stone engraving representing a phallus, Perigordian VI, Laugerie-Haute, about 21,000 B.C.* **National Museum of Prehistory at Les Eyzies.**

ric chronology, thanks to its 42 sedimentary levels whose vast outlier layers are shown to the public. It was occupied from the end of the Gravettian (23,000 B.C.), but is above all

*Laugerie-Haute: female "vulva" sexual symbol, engraved in stone, Perigordian VI.* **National Museum of Prehistory at Les Eyzies.**

*Horned animal engraved on a block of stone, Laugerie-Haute, Magdalenian III, about 15,000 years old.* **National Museum of Prehistory at Les Eyzies.**

typical of the Solutrean (20,000 to 17,000 B.C.) and possesses the whole stratigraphic series. It was abandoned in the Magdalenian after the collapse of its upper terrace, (around 14,000 B.C.). Before that, it formed one of the biggest shelters in France, 200 metres (220 yds) long and 35 metres (40 yds) deep. It was excavated by Lartet and Christy in 1863 and then by many others, including Capitan in 1895, Peyrony in 1921, Bordes in 1955 and Geneviève Guichard from 1968 to 1988. It contains several animal engravings dating from the Solutrean period. A Neolithic tomb was found to the west.

The Richard cave (or Eyzies cave), near the museum, provided the discoveries which were the origin of the first modern archeological excavations, in 1862. It was occupied

*A shingle stone engraved with geometrical signs, Laugerie-Haute, Perigordian VII.* **National Museum of Prehistory at Les Eyzies.**

from the Solutrean period, but its deposits of colouring materials belonged to the artists of the Middle Magdalenian (12,000 B.C.). It was still inhabited in Azilian times. Among other art works, two pendants decorated with a wolverine and four horses were found there.

*Prehistoric dwellings at Laugerie-Basse: Les Marseilles shelter, stratigraphic section.* Photo Delon.

***Laugerie-Basse : a fine Magdalenian site***

Situated at the foot of spectacular cliffs, the first shelter of the Laugerie-Basse prehistoric site, open to visitors, contained many tools from the Middle or Upper Magdalenian, and from the Azilian, that is 12,000 to 8,000 B.C. It was excavated by Lartet in 1864.

The second shelter, the Marseilles, covers a wider period. The whole of the Magdalenian, from 15,000 to 10,000 B.C. is present here. It is contemporary with the great artistic achievements of Les Eyzies (Font-de-Gaume, Combarelles etc.). Its final layer belongs to Neolithic times (5,000 B.C.) and the end of the Bronze Age. A block of stone engraved with low-reliefs from the Magdalenian was found here. The site was then occupied by a troglodyte village. A small museum displays the finds from the site. Laugerie-Basse has revealed some surprising works of art, such as the immodest Venus and the lady with the reindeer.

But there are yet other shelters at Les Eyzies, where each patch of ground holds traces of the past. Many others should be mentioned: La Liveyre, Casserole, and Guilhem shelters, and count-

***Prehistoric dwellings at Laugerie-Basse: modern troglodyte houses.***
Photo Lasvenes.

less sites: La Combe, Le Biscot, Esclafer, Malbarrat, Peyrille, Le Tunnel, Souffron, Vidal etc. This inventory is not complete, but other sites from neighbouring communes must be mentioned: Le Bugue, Rouffignac, Sireuil, Tursac, Meyrals. These will be studied separately to avoid an "overdose" of Prehistory.

***Stalagmite columns and small canopy. Carpe-Diem cave (Manaurie).***
Photo J. Bouscaillou.

## Tayac and the concretions caves of Grand-Roc and Carpe-Diem

We return to historic times to visit the Tayac church, built as a fortress by the monks of Paunat abbey in the XIIth century. The windows are in fact no more than loopholes. The East end and the main wall are each surmounted by a keep topped with *lauzes*, or stone slates. The portal has five recessed arches of Limousin style. The east end with its walls 2.5 metres (8 ft.) thick and the capitals of the portal show re-use of the pre-romanesque. The crenellated terrace of the east end, the defensive redoubt of the west wall, and the majestic and pure elevations contribute to classifying the church of Tayac as one of the most beautiful fortress-churches of Périgord.

On the other bank of the Vézère, the Roc de Tayac was first of all a troglodyte fort before becoming a fortress and a toll-post for bargees in the early Middle Ages. Transformed into an "aerial restaurant" at the beginning of the century, it now houses the museum of Speleology. On display there are explorers' equipment, specimens of cave fauna, everything accompanied by detailed explanatory diagrams.

Niched among the prehistoric sites, above Laugerie-Basse, one can visit the Grand-Roc cave with its concretions. This was discovered in 1924 and has very beautiful "eccentrics" resembling corals. The abundance of crystals, and the wealth of the shapes and colours make it a real jewel... seen from inside.

On the Périgueux road, after Laugerie-Haute, there is another cave with concretions at Manaurie, which is also open to visitors. This is Carpe-Diem, with its coloured stalactites. Another excavation, the Ourtalou cave, is not open to the public. On the Rouffignac road, one can see the Roc de Pépue on which Peyrony thought he saw prehistoric engravings, which turned out to be due to erosion phenomena.

*Grand-Roc cliff.*

***Carpe-Diem cave (Manaurie).***
Photo J. Bouscaillou.

***Bouquet of eccentrics. Grand-Roc cave.***
Photo Repérant.

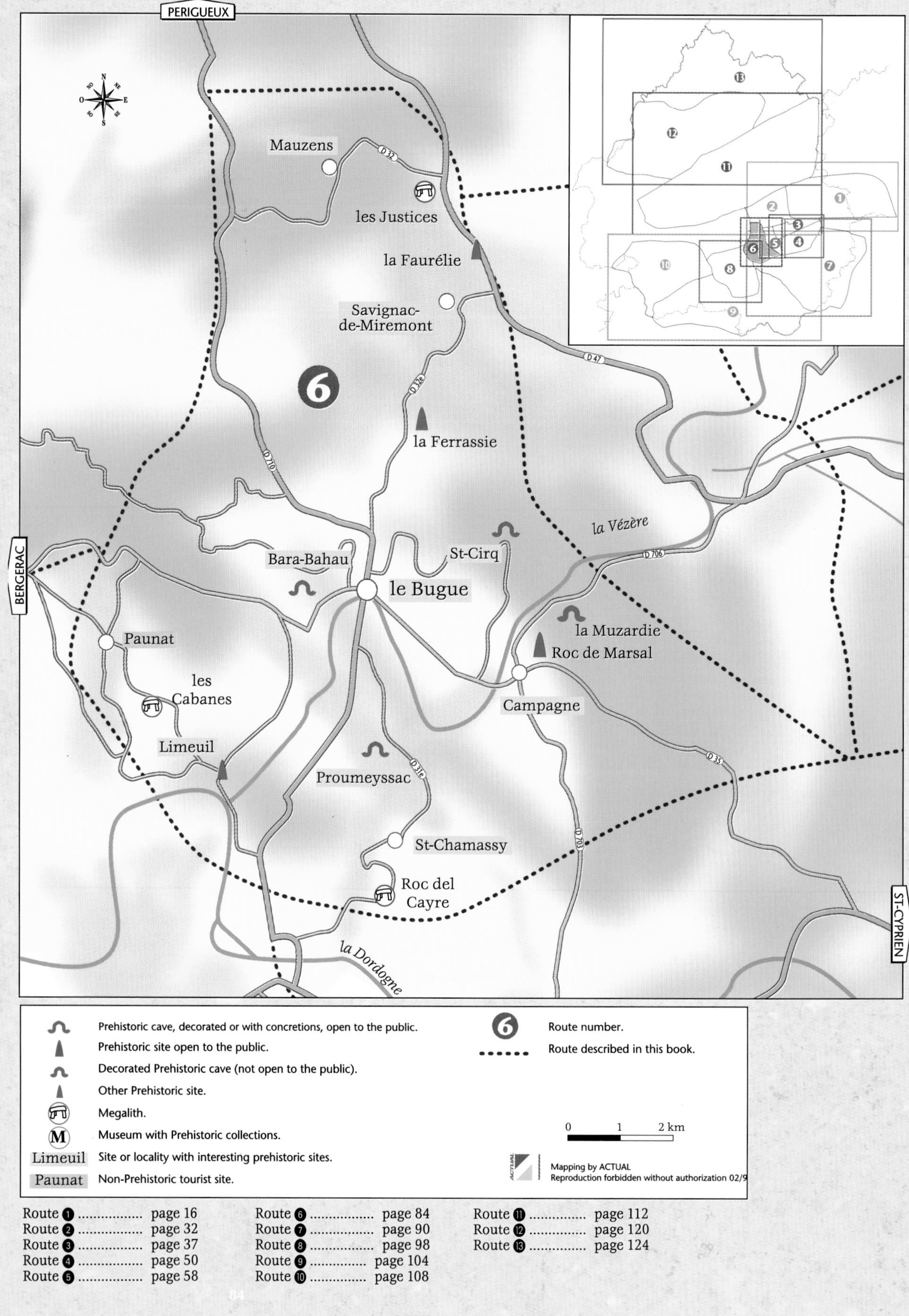
PERIGUEUX
BERGERAC
ST-CYPRIEN
Mauzens
D 32
les Justices
la Faurélie
Savignac-
de-Miremont
D 47
D 32e
6
la Ferrassie
D 710
la Vézère
St-Cirq
D 706
Bara-Bahau
le Bugue
la Muzardie
Roc de Marsal
Paunat
les
Cabanes
Campagne
Limeuil
D 35
Proumeyssac
D 31e
St-Chamassy
D 703
Roc del
Cayre
la Dordogne
Prehistoric cave, decorated or with concretions, open to the public.
Prehistoric site open to the public.
Decorated Prehistoric cave (not open to the public).
Other Prehistoric site.
Megalith.
Museum with Prehistoric collections.
Limeuil Site or locality with interesting prehistoric sites.
Paunat Non-Prehistoric tourist site.
Route number.
Route described in this book.
0 1 2 km
Mapping by ACTUAL
Reproduction forbidden without authorization 02/9

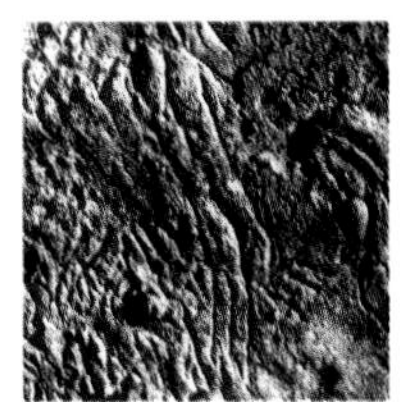

# Around Le Bugue

## Le Bugue, the western door to Prehistory: Saint-Cirq, Bara-Bahau and Proumeyssac

Route 6

*Tortoise from Saint-Cirq-du-Bugue.*

### Saint-Cirq and La Ferrassie

Downstream from Les Eyzies, the river Vézère continues on its way through Prehistory. Five kilometres (3 miles) from Les Eyzies, there is a prehistoric cave open for visits in the little village of Saint-Cirq-du-Bugue, called the cave of Vic or Le Sorcier (Sorcerer). It was discovered in 1952 by Mortureux, from the town of Sarlat, and he was joined by Abbé Breuil. It contains several dozen engravings dating back to 13,000 B.C., including a very fine dappled horse and an exceptional representation of a man with a complete and human face. This engraving was the first to show what Mag-

**Sites open to visitors near Bugue**

*__Proumeyssac__ chasm (concretions), tel. 05.53.07.27.47.*
*__Bara-Bahau__ cave, tel. 05.53.07.27.47.*
*__Saint-Cirq__ cave (and museum), tel. 05.53.07.14.37.*
*__La Ferrassie__ prehistoric site, tel. 05.53.06.90.80.*
*__Campagne__ museum.*
*__Bugue__ Tourist Office, tel. 05.53.07.20.48.*
*__Limeuil__ Tourist Bureau, tel. 05.53.63.38.90.*

*Walkers will take the GR6 which links Les Eyzies, Saint-Cirq, Le Bugue and Limeuil. Do not miss the fine abbey church of Paunat.*

*In Bugue: aquarium, village of Bournat, museum of Palaeontology, wildlife house.*

*Dug-out cave shelters at Saint-Cirq-du-Bugue.*

*Opposite page: Bara-Bahau. From top to bottom: engraved bear. The numerous traces of the presence of bears in this cave in ancient times, while the representation of this animal by prehistoric artists is very rare, make Bara-Bahau the bear-cave sanctuary;*

*scratches made by bear-claws;*

*engraved hand.*
Site photo.

dalenian man looked like. He resembles a modern man, but somewhat obese. To this day, it is one the best human engravings of cave wall art. Near the cave, a little museum displays local finds. Apart from the prehistoric shelter, one can visit the troglodyte fort of Pech Saint-Sourd which has several underground galleries and dug-out cave shelters. Poised on the cliff, with a surprising tuft of bamboo on top, the site has great charm.

*Representation of a man, called "The Sorcerer" from Saint-Cirq-du-Bugue.*

Five kilometres (3 miles) north of Bugue, at Savignac-de-Miremont, the three prehistoric sites of La Ferrassie, one of which can be seen from the road, present a very good example of stratigraphy. Beginning in 1896, they were excavated by many prehistorians, in particular D. Peyrony. The very special lithic industry of this site allowed F. Bordes to define five types of Mousterian tools. The oldest level, Mousterian of Acheulian tradition, is 100,000 years old and has revealed several Neanderthal graves. Eight skeletons, two adults and six children, are proof of the existence of elaborate funeral rites even at this epoch. In the upper levels, one finds Châtelperronian, Aurignacian with a few stone blocks engraved with archaic figures, and Perigordian. At Mauzens-Mirement, the La Faurélie shelter, discovered in 1958, was inhabited in the Upper Magdalenian period. Finds include spears, needles with eyes, and a necklace of shells. One can also see the Justices' polisher, where Neolithic men came to polish their axes 6,000 years ago.

### Campagne, Le Bugue and Bara-Bahau

The village of Campagne-du-Bugue has a superb castle, surrounded by a vast park and overlooked by a rocky massif, a former oppidum, a rocky spur pierced with many shelters and containing the prehistoric sites of Poulverouze and the Roc de Marsal. On the flank of the cliff, the ruins of a troglodyte fort and hamlet still remain. In 1961, the skeleton of a Neanderthal child was found at the Roc de Marsal, buried in a tomb. The commune also includes the prehistoric site of La Vergnole and, on the road to Saint-Cyprien, that of Péchalifour. In the castle of Campagne, over 3,000 square metres (3,600 sq. yds) are to be devoted to a store and depository for archeologi-

***Head of an auroch deeply engraved in the soft rock. Bara-Bahau.***
Site photo.

cal finds. It will be open to the public, and its park developed. On the Les Eyzies road, in the La Muzardie cave the dome of a skull was found. It is decorated with several engravings, including a horse, dating from Magdalenian times.

The welcoming village of Le Bugue, surrounded by wooded hills and built on terraces on the right bank of a bend in the Vézère river, can be called the "golden door to Prehistory". With its 3,000 inhabitants, it is one of the major localities of Périgord Noir.

One kilometre (half a mile) to the north-west, one finds the Bara-Bahau cave, discovered in 1951 by the speleologist Norbert Casteret. This cavern, 100 metres long (110 yds), is open to the public. The rock is brittle and soft (Abbé Glory compared it to cottage cheese), and prehistoric artists used their fingers, flints or sticks to engrave mysterious tectiform signs and silhouettes of aurochs, bears, bison, ibex and horses. The very rustic style of these works makes it difficult to date them. Abbé Breuil thought, wrongly, that they were the very beginnings of art. These days they are considered to be from the early Magdalenian period (15,000 B.C.).

***Descent into the Proumeyssac chasm in a basket, just like the first explorers at the beginning of the XXth century.***
Site photo.

## The Proumeyssac chasm and Limeuil

Three kilometres (2 miles) to the south, the Proumeyssac chasm can be visited. For many years it was thought to be a volcano because of the vapours it emitted. Over the centuries, brigands and other bandits threw the bodies of travellers they had robbed down there. This enormous hole, 80 metres in diameter (90 yds), was closed and left to sleep by Bailiff Jean-Baptiste Pélissier du Barry, in the XVIIIth century. It was only reopened in 1901, and explored using a suspended basket. A tunnel was bored in 1957, so that it can now be reached without difficulty. One discovers a sink-hole with concretions nearly 50 metres (165 ft.) high, a great number of translucid stalactites (still alive because of a little stream running through), "eccentrics" in strange shapes, a petrifying fountain and very peculiar triangular crystallizations. The Proumeyssac chasm, according to Norbert Casteret, is "amongst the finest jewels of subterranean France".

The village of Limeuil, perched above the confluence of the Vézère and the Dordogne rivers, is full of charm and poetry. According to Eugène Le Roy, the view from the esplanade of the castle is "the finest in Périgord". The hill was inhabited in prehistoric times. Situated below the village, the extensive Limeuil prehistoric site, dating from the Upper Magdalenian (10,000 B.C.) and excavated as early as 1909 by Abbés Breuil and Bouyssonie, has provided about 200 plaques covered with engravings of reindeer and horses. At a time, A. Leroi-Gourhan thought it was a sanctuary with mobile elements. It could have been an art school. The neighbouring site of Font-Brunel dates from the end of the Magdalenian. Three kilometres (2 miles) from Limeuil, at Soulalève, is the Lestruque cave, which was discovered in 1929 and contained reindeer antlers sculpted with reindeer heads, dating from the Magdalenian period.

A little to the south, near Saint-Chamassy, at Brandes, the fine dolmen of the Roc del Cayre (or Cantegrel) dominates the Dordogne valley. A headless skeleton was found beneath it. Another dolmen can be found further north, at Paunat, Les Cabanes.

***General view of the Proumeyssac chasm.***
Site photo.

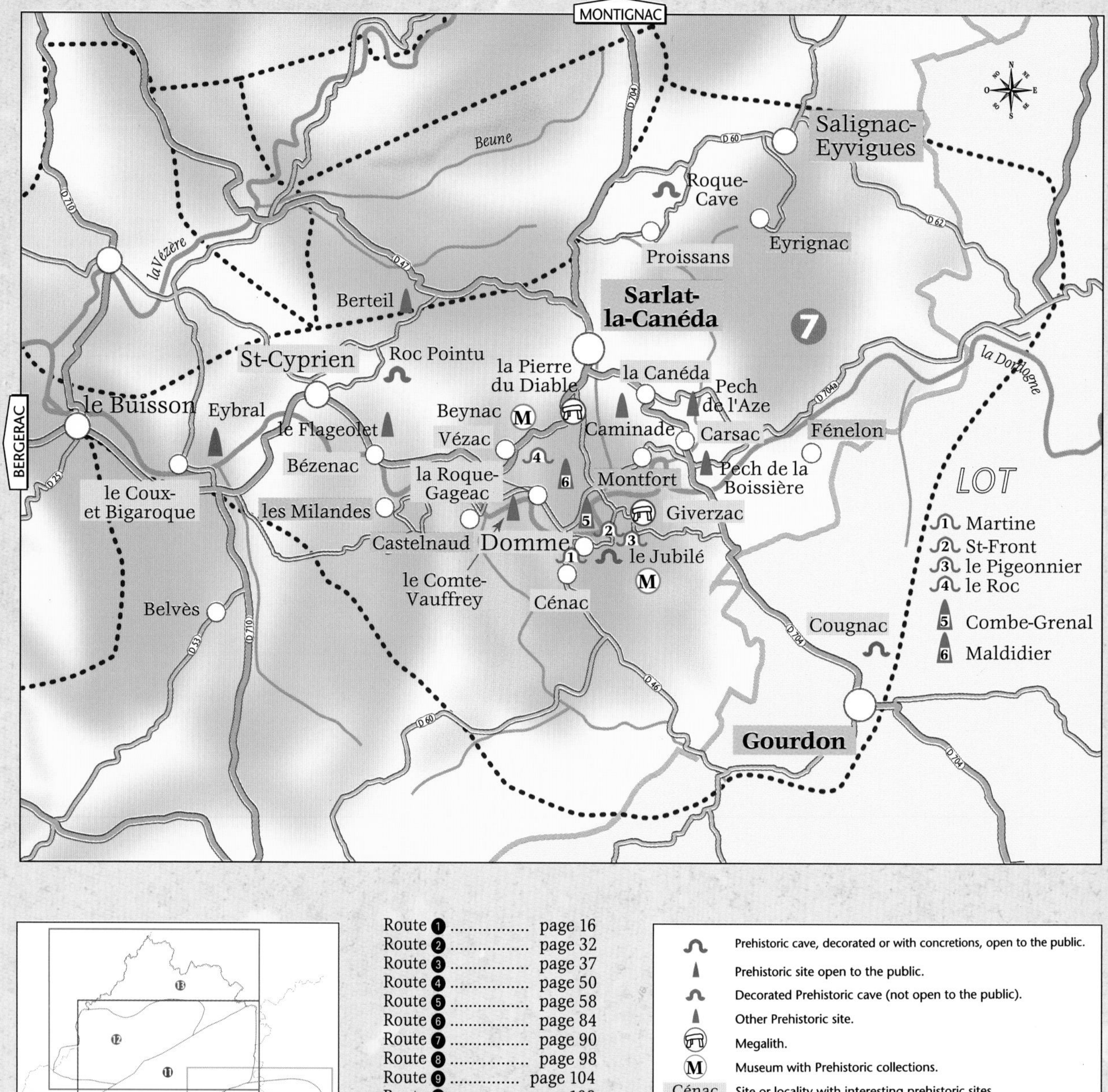

MONTIGNAC
Salignac-
Eyvigues
D 60
Beune
D 704
Roque-
Cave
Eyrignac
D 62
Proissans
D 710
la Vézère
D 47
Berteil
Sarlat-
la-Canéda
7
la Dordogne
St-Cyprien
Roc Pointu
la Pierre
du Diable
la Canéda
Pech
de l'Aze
D 704a
BERGERAC
le Buisson
Eybral
Beynac
le Flageolet
Caminade
Carsac
Fénelon
Vézac
Bézenac
la Roque-
Gageac
Montfort
Pech de la
Boissière
LOT
le Coux-
et Bigaroque
les Milandes
Giverzac
D 25
Castelnaud
Domme
le Jubilé
le Comte-
Vauffrey
Cénac
1 Martine
2 St-Front
3 le Pigeonnier
4 le Roc
5 Combe-Grenal
6 Maldidier
Belvès
Cougnac
D 53
D 710
D 704
D 46
D 60
Gourdon
D 704

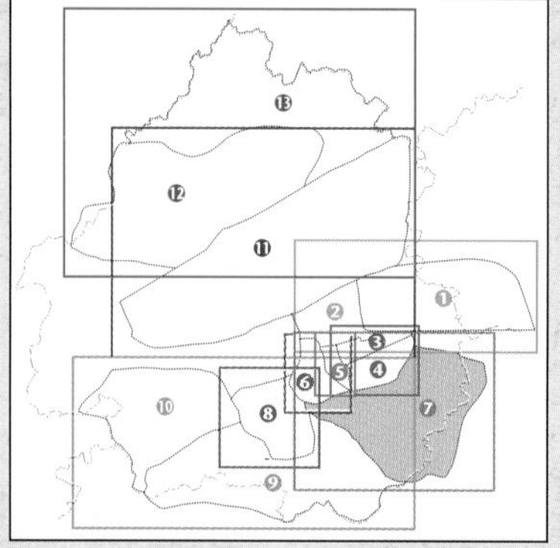



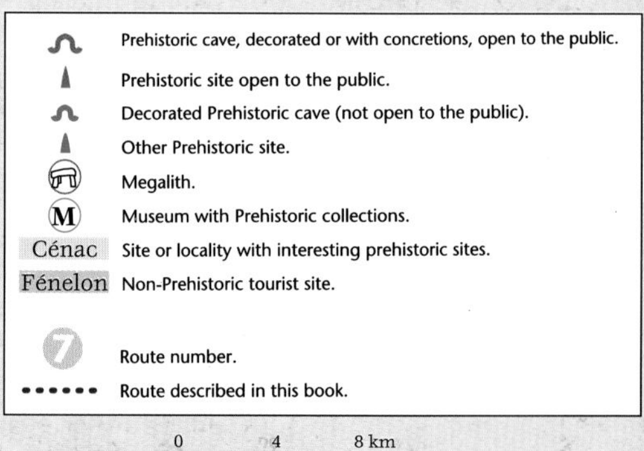

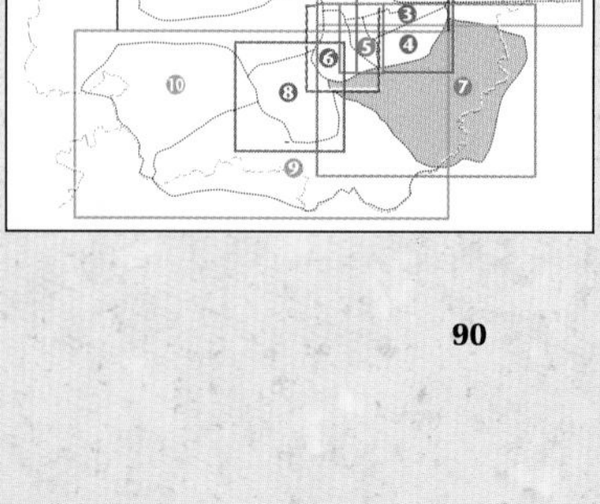

0 4 8 km

Mapping by ACTUAL

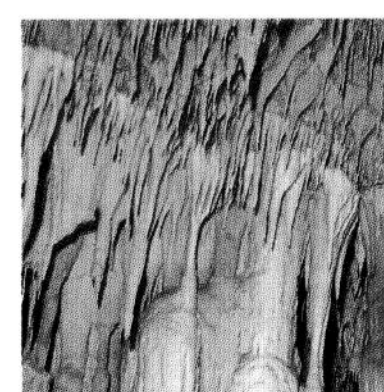

# Around Sarlat

## THE DORDOGNE VALLEY AROUND SARLAT, IN PÉRIGORD NOIR

Route 7

### Sarlat country and the dawn of humanity: le Pech de l'Aze

Sarlat, the tourist capital of Périgord has prehistoric remains itself: the Cantelouve shelter and the Pierre du Diable dolmen (Devil's dolmen) where the inhabitants of Sarlat, who thought they saw the scratches of the claws of Satan there, burned the bodies of their lepers. A Sarlat museum is to open in the Plamon house, in the heart of the old town. Proissans, apart from a strange megalith, on the Salignac road, has a cave-shelter, the Roque-Cave, engraved with a quadrangular sign. At La Canéda, the Caminade shelter, partly collapsed, was excavated in 1953 by G. Mortureux and D. de Sonneville-Bordes. It was

*Sarlat: the Pierre du Diable dolmen.*

**Sites open to visitors near Sarlat and Domme**

***Cougnac*** *cave, tel. 05.65.41.47.54.*
***Jubilé*** *cave (Domme)*
***Paul-Reclus*** *cave (Domme)*
***Beynac Protohistory*** *museum, tel. 05.53.29.51.28.*
***Eybral*** *sepulchre-cave,* ***at Coux.***

***Sarlat*** *Tourist Office, tel. 05.53.59.27.67.*
***Domme*** *Tourist Office, tel. 05.53.28.37.09.*

***Gourdon*** *Tourist Office, tel. 05.65.41.06.40.*
***Beynac*** *Tourist Bureau, tel. 05.53.29.43.08.*
***Saint-Cyprien*** *Tourist Bureau, tel. 05.53.30.36.09.*
***Siorac*** *Tourist Bureau, tel. 05.53.31.63.51.*
***Carlux*** *Tourist Bureau, tel. 05.53.29.71.08.*
***Salignac*** *Tourist Bureau, tel. 05.53.28.81.93.*

*The GR 6 leads the walker from Sarlat to Carsac, and then the GR 64A follows the course of the Dordogne from Montfort to Saint-Cyprien. The 36-64 then rejoins Les Eyzies. The castles of Salignac, Eyrignac, Fénelon, Montfort, Beynac, Castelnaud and Milandes are open to the public. Do not miss the medieval village of Sarlat, the fortified town of Domme and the village of La Roque-Gageac.*

*One can also recommend the view from the Dordogne river in a canoe; cliffs topped by castles.*

1

2

## *Acheulian*

*The Acheulian era (named after Saint-Acheul in the Somme) is the principal cultural facies of the lower Palaeolithic. In Périgord, it lasted from 450,000 to 100,000 B.C. Homo erectus and then the first Homo sapiens who inhabited our lands at that time, could master fire and carve biface tools. We do not know whether they had funeral rites. In Périgord, the prehistoric site of La Micoque, at Les Eyzies, and the Pech de l'Aze and Vauffrey caves, in the Dordogne valley, provide evidence of this distant past.*

***From 1 to 8: Knapping flints: Beginning with a block of silex, Pascal Rau chips off a splinter using a striker, then shapes it with a box-wood hammer.***

occupied in Mousterian and Aurignacian times, and has given its name to the type of scraper used in the latter epoch.

At Carsac, apart from the Roc d'Abeille (Bee) shelter, one should also mention the Pech de la Boissière site, excavated by Peyrony, and occupied by Solutrean man (20,000 to 15,000 B.C.), who left behind him an impressive lithic industry (his "laurel leaves" can be counted among the most beautiful and the biggest of Prehistory, reaching 27 centimetres, 10.5 inches, in length for 7 to 8 millimetres, about 0.3 inches, in width), and stones engraved

3

4

5

6

7

8

with animals. The upper level dates from the early Magdalenian.

The road between Sarlat and Gourdon, before Carsac, follows the huge Mousterian shelter of the Pech de l'Aze, comprising four caves and rock-shelters. It was one of the first sites excavated (in 1816 by F. Jouannet), and was examined again in 1909 by Capitan and D. Peyrony, who found the skull of a Neanderthal child there. Further excavations in 1950 by Bordes defined five Mousterian levels of Acheulian culture and found colouring materials, ochre and manganese dioxide, used by Neanderthal man. For which works of art, no longer here today, were they intended? In a second cave, under seven Mousterian levels, rhinoceros bones were discovered and an Acheulian layer from 300,000 to 400,000 years ago. Traces of hearths prove that fire had been mastered at this time.

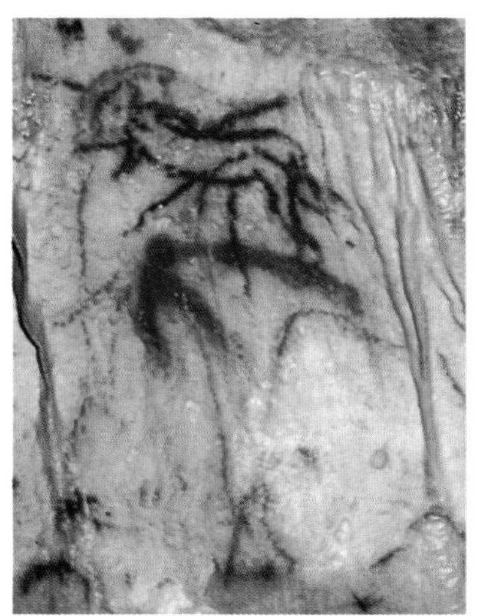

*Cougnac cave (Lot).*

## The Cougnac cave, near Gourdon

We now leave Périgord for a few kilometres, to visit the magnificent Cougnac caves, open to visitors, just before Gourdon, in the Payrignac commune. They are comprised of two distinct cavities, decorated by nature long before Man appeared, a fairyland of fluorescent concretions. Thousands of slim stalactites adorn the ceilings of the first cave. 17,000 years ago, Magdalenian artists had to break through stalactites and stalagmites to paint the walls of the second cave. This was only discovered in 1949, thanks to radiesthesia, and according to Leroi-Gourhan, its decoration is unusual since it is composed essentially of male signs. Among 300 motifs, one can see three giant stags, a megaloceros, and two men pierced by spears. The style of the drawings

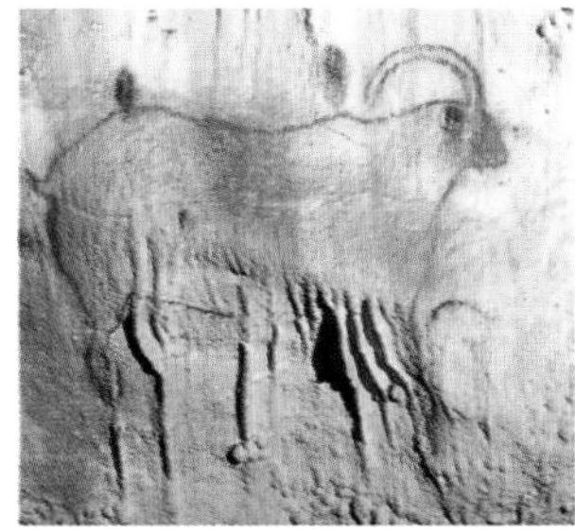

***Ibex.***
***Cougnac.***

***A man pierced by an arrow.***
***Cougnac.***
Photo F. Jach.

***Beynac archaeological park.*** Site photo.

is reminiscent of the Pech-Merle cave (near Cahors, open to the public).

## Following the Dordogne, around Domme

***Domme and the Jubilé cave***

Apart from the Salcets dolmen, above the troglodyte chapel of Caudon, Vitrac has two fine sink-holes carved out by the river. Not far away, the Redoulet cave with concretions extends for 1,300 metres (1,420 yds).

The Dordogne valley has few prehistoric remains known to the general public. Nonetheless, Domme is one of the most important prehistoric centres in Périgord. The American writer Henry Miller compared the Domme Acropolis to paradise on earth: (...) a paradise which must have existed for thousands and thousands of years. I am convinced that for Cro-Magnon man it was this. There is nothing to stop me believing that if Cro-Magnon man settled here it was because he was extremely intelligent, with a highly developed sense of beauty".

In the town centre, the XVIIth century covered market hides the entrance to the Jubilé concretions cave, open to the public. It is 450 metres (490 yds) long, and is a fairyland world of white stalactites and stalagmites. Bison and mammoth bones were found during construction of the entrance corridor. The Domme caves were frequented by Palaeolithic man, who left behind him several engravings which are almost unreadable, and served as a refuge for the local inhabitants during troubled times. The Paul-Reclus museum is devoted to finds from the Domme and in particular Prehistory with an interesting collection of Mousterian tools.

The Combe-Grenal cave, at the foot of the cliffs, was excavated by Jouannet in 1816, by Peyrony in 1891, and by Bordes

***After excavations, reconstitution of Gaulish houses. Beynac archaeological park.***
Site photo.

in 1953. It comprises 64 archeological levels on 10 metres (32 ft.). One can see 28 Mousterian levels, containing four of the five facies of this epoch. A small round ditch was found, 70,000 years old and, among Quina-type tools, a child's jawbone. The Martine cave, below the town of Domme, discovered in 1963, contains animal paintings and engravings dating back to the Magdalenian, and remains from the Bronze and Iron Ages. In the Saint-Front hamlet, the Saint-Front cave, or Mammoth cave, discovered in 1978, has produced various tools from Perigordian times and, among other engravings, a very fine low-relief sculpture of a mammoth dating back to early Magdalenian times. The neighbouring Pigeonnier cave, discovered in the same year, contains engravings of animals from the same epoch. Near Domme, but of more recent prehistory, one can see a dolmen at the entrance to the Giverzac castle.

***Weaving class, one of the many workshops open to school groups. Beynac archaeological park.***
Site photo.

### *Between Vaufrey and Eybral, the museum of Protohistory of Beynac*

The de Vaufrey cave shelter, next to the medieval castle of Castelnaud, at Cénac, was discovered in 1930 and excavated between 1969 and 1981 by J.-Ph. Rigaud, who found Mousterian and Acheulian tools and choppers (rough tools of the pebble culture). This site is essential to the study of the appearance of

***Teaching workshop. Beynac archaeological park.*** Site photo.

Mousterian industry. Vaufrey, which is only one of the many caves in the Comte cliff, contained pottery and burial places from the middle Bronze Age.

***Pottery workshop. Beynac archaeological park.*** Site photo.

Near the pretty village of La Roque-Gageac, whose cliff is reflected in the green waters of the Dordogne, the small Maldidier cave holds Aurignacian and Perigordian remains. According to J.-Ph. Rigaud, who excavated it, it could have been occupied from time to time by hunters chasing fur animals. Below, the Roc de Vézac cave is interesting because of the total absence of animal representations. Punctuation points, negative hands and two strange reniform signs (kidney-shaped) were probably produced at the end of the Aurignacian period (25,000 B.C.). If we continue our descent of the river we reach Beynac, which has just opened a museum of

*Prehistoric excavations, Le Flageolet at Bézenac.*

Protohistory in the castle. Between 5,000 and 50 B.C., the hunter became a farmer and towns started to develop. This was the Roman Conquest, which brought Gaul into History.

Further on, at Bézenac, the two Flageolet caves were excavated by J.-Ph. Rigaud between 1967 and 1984. The first shelter was occupied in the Aurignacian era from 32,000 B.C. and then in the Perigordian epoch. Flageolet II contains Magdalenian remains. At Castels, near Saint-Cyprien, the Roc-Pointu (pointed rock) cave was discovered in 1975. It is decorated with a fine bison's head, difficult to date. High up above the town, the vast Berteil oppidum, which walls in the summit of the hill, was already inhabited in Neolithic times. At Coux, the Eybral sepulchre-cave also dates from the Neolithic. The site includes a museum. The collective tomb holds 80 skeletons, some of them burned, dating from late Neolithic times (3,000 B.C.). One skull shows traces of two trepannings, which the individual had survived. A bronze dagger was also found at Coux.

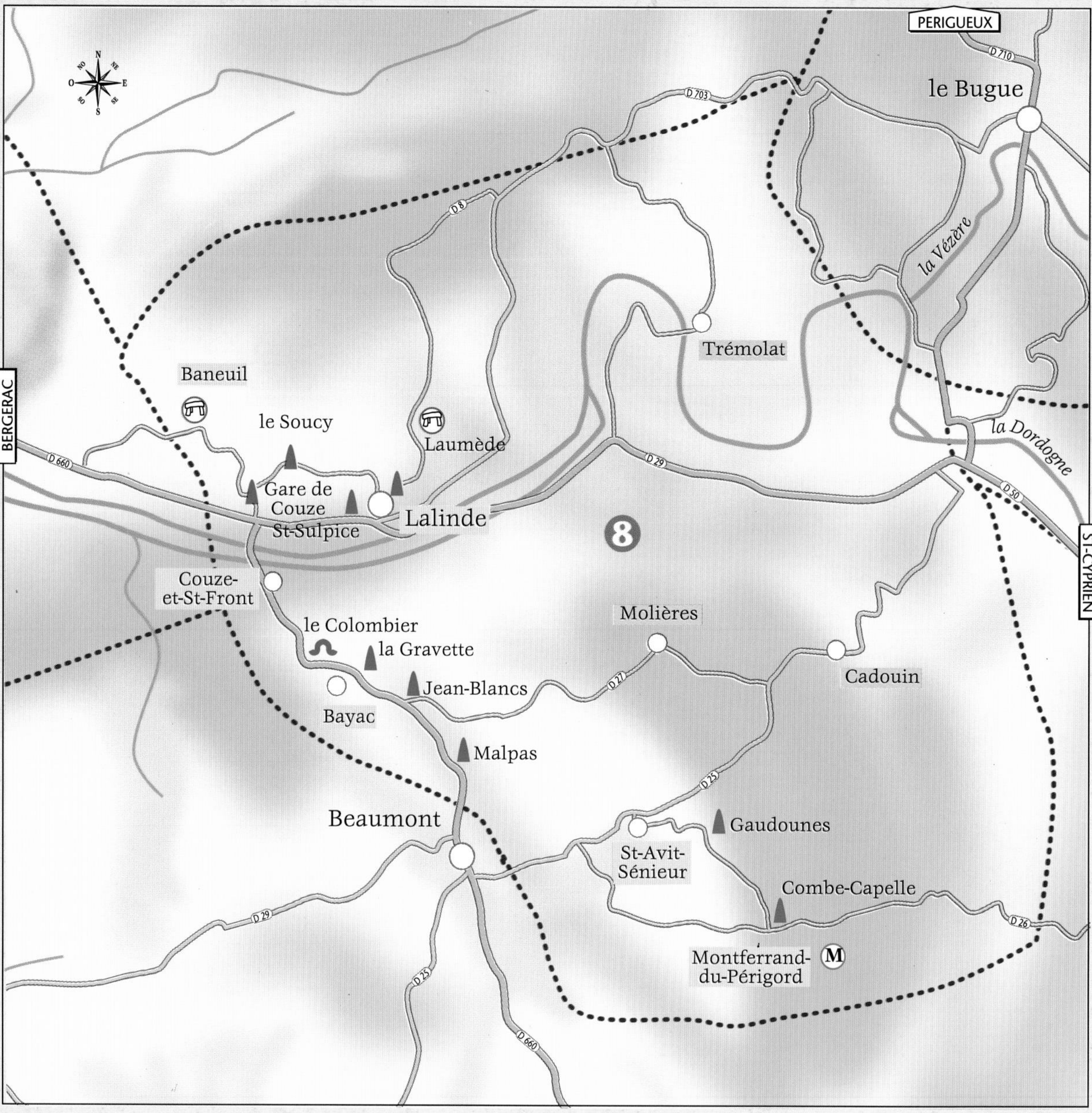

PERIGUEUX
D 710
le Bugue
D 703
D 8
la Vézère
Trémolat
Baneuil
BERGERAC
le Soucy
Laumède
D 660
Gare de
Couze
St-Sulpice
Lalinde
D 29
la Dordogne
D 50
ST-CYPRIEN
8
Couze-
et-St-Front
le Colombier
la Gravette
Molières
Cadouin
Jean-Blancs
D 27
Bayac
Malpas
D 25
Beaumont
Gaudounes
St-Avit-
Sénieur
Combe-Capelle
D 26
D 29
Montferrand-
du-Périgord
M
D 25
D 660

Prehistoric cave, decorated or with concretions, open to the public.
Prehistoric site open to the public.
Decorated Prehistoric cave (not open to the public).
Other Prehistoric site.
Megalith.
M Museum with Prehistoric collections.
Bayac Site or locality with interesting prehistoric sites.
Cadouin Non-Prehistoric tourist site.
8 Route number.
Route described in this book.
0 2 4 km

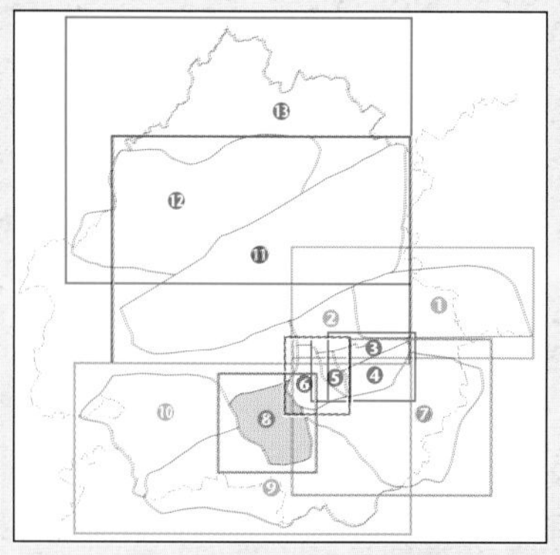

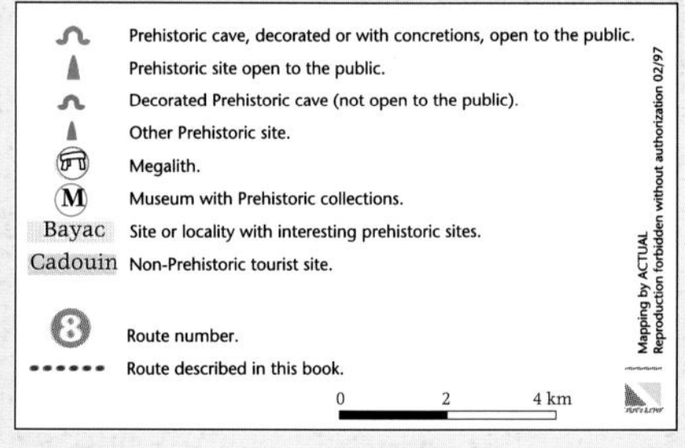

# From Montferrand to Lalinde

**THE COUZE VALLEY, FROM MONTFERRAND TO LALINDE**

Route 8

## Saint-Avit-Sénieur and Montferrand

In the south of the *départe-ment*, the Couze valley is little known but is a prehistoric centre of great importance. Far from the normal tourist circuits, the stream follows 25 kilometres (15 miles) peacefully through "Bastide country" (walled towns).

Apart from its splendid fortified church, Saint-Avit-Sénieur

***Near Lalinde, the Dordogne, the other Prehistory river, after the Vézère.***

### Sites open to visitors in the Couze valley

*__Montferrand-du-Périgord__ museum*
*Project for a __Couze valley__ museum*
*__Buisson__ Tourist Bureau, tel. 05.53.22.06.09.*
*__Lalinde__ Tourist Bureau, tel. 05.53.61.08.55.*
*__Trémolat__ Tourist Bureau, tel. 05.53.22.89.33.*

*The GR 6E reveals the beauties of the valley to those on foot: the village of Saint-Croix, the Saint-Avit-Sénieur church, Bannes castle, the Bayac and Couze sites (paper museum), the Lalinde bastide. Also see Cadouin abbey and the church at Trémolat.*

*Gorge d'Enfer (Les Eyzies): The Poisson (Fish) shelter. This salmon, 44 inches long, dates from around 23,000 B.C. and is one of the rare representations known of a fish in cave-wall art.*

possesses many traces of a far-off past. The best known are the two prehistoric sites of Combe-Capelle. In 1909, at the Combe-Capelle rock, Hauser discovered a Châtelperronian sepulchre under Solutrean, Gravettian and Aurignacian layers. It dated from 35,000 B.C. and contained a skeleton with shell necklaces, of a human being similar to Cro-Magnon man but still possessing several characteristics of Neanderthal man. Combe-Capelle man was displayed in the Berlin museum before the war, but was destroyed in the bombing of 1944. He was the oldest *Homo sapiens sapiens* known, our very own ancestor in a way. Combe-Capelle made it possible for D. Peyrony to define early Perigordian, and for Breuil to understand better the change from Perigordian to Solutrean. The upper site at Combe-Capelle contains Mousterian of Acheulian tradition, from thousands of centuries ago. In the same commune one also finds the prehistoric sites of Patary and Fontaine-de-Gaudounes. Thermo-Pialat contained a plaque with two female representations from Aurignacian times.

On the other side of the valley, one can go and see the village of Montferrand-du-Périgord, rich in Mousterian sites of Acheulian tradition, and a small museum (in the town hall) devoted to the Prehistory of the Couze valley.

## Bayac, the Gravettian capital

Bayac is the prehistoric capital of the Couze valley. When one arrives in the village, the Gravette site, which gave its name to Gravettian, was excavated as early as 1880. It revealed two Aurignacian levels (the second, characterized by small leaf-like points, was formerly called Bayacian) and three Gravettian levels where they discovered many small points with straight edges: the Gravette points. It was in the Gravettian, or recent Perigordian period, that Cro-Magnon man perfected the art of engraving and, for example, created the magnificent salmon in the Gorge d'Enfer at Les Eyzies and most of the prehistoric Venuses. There are several prehistoric sites around Bayac: Mazerat, Colombier (small decorated cave), La Cavaille and Le Malpas.

Between Bayac and Bourniquel, the two Jean-Blancs (or Champs-Blancs) shelters were excavated in 1912 by Bouyssonie and Peyrony, who revealed a splendid Solutrean lithic industry and several engraved stone blocks from the early Magdalenian period (present excavations by J.-J. Clayet-Merle). There is a plan to set up a Couze valley museum.

### Female representations from Lalinde and Couze-et-Saint-Front

At the confluence of the Couze and the Dordogne, one finds the village of Couze-et-Saint-Front, partly troglodyte, climbing up from the water's edge to the top of the slope. Apart from the Peyrol prehistoric hole, the commune also holds the Gare-de-Couze site, comprising a cave, two shelters and an open-air dwelling. The site was studied by Peyrony and then by Bordes, and revealed a plaque engraved with female representations dating from the Upper Magdalenian (on display in the Les Eyzies museum), and gave its name to a microlith: the Couze rectangle.

The Lalinde bastide, or fortified town, bordered by the Dordogne, comprises several prehistoric sites: Saint-Sulpice-des-Magnats and especially La Roche at Lalinde, which contained a flat stone covered with female representations, dating from the recent Magdalenian period (10,000 B.C.). A copy is on display in the museum at Les Eyzies. The Soucy shelter, discovered in 1881, is a major site from the Upper Magdalenian, confirmed by an extensive lithic and bone industry, and rich in portable art, including the famous "churinga", one of the rare musical instruments known. For megalith enthusiasts, there are the Laumède and Baneuil dolmens, near the village town hall. An English general is said to be buried underneath.

### Châtelperronian and Gravettien

*Between 35,000 and 30,000 B.C., the Châtelperronian period, named by Abbé Breuil after the Châtelperron site, in the Allier, marks the transition between the Mousterian and the Upper Palaeolithic. It was during this mysterious period that modern man replaced Neanderthal man, without any real rupture of industry. In Périgord, one finds this situation at Combe-Capelle, La Ferrassie and Le Moustier.*
*After the Aurignacian period, which saw the triumph of the Cro-Magnon civilization, came the Gravettian (25,000 to 17,000 B.C.) which was characterized by remarkable sculptures: the Venus of Laussel, and the salmon in the Poisson (fish) cave. La Gravette, La Ferrassie and Laugerie-Haute are demonstrations of important stratigraphs of this epoch.*

**La Roche at Lalinde: engraved block of stone with female representations. Magdalenian. National Museum of Prehistory at Les Eyzies.**

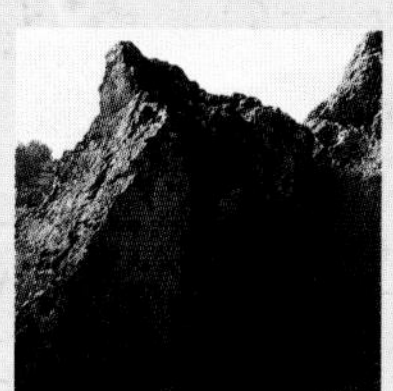

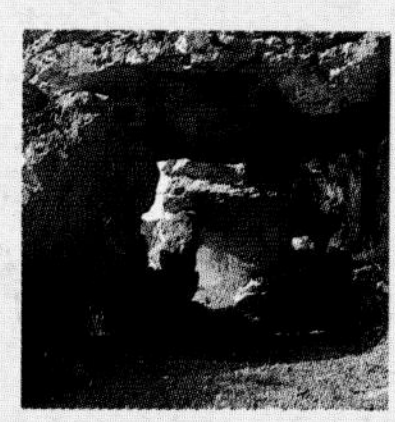

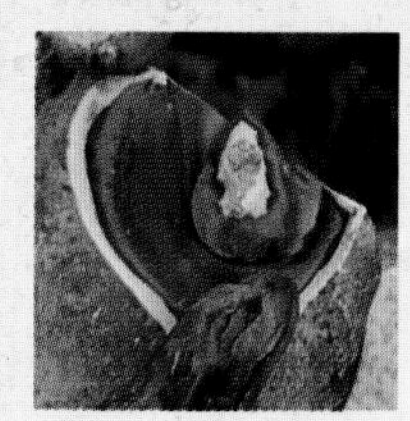

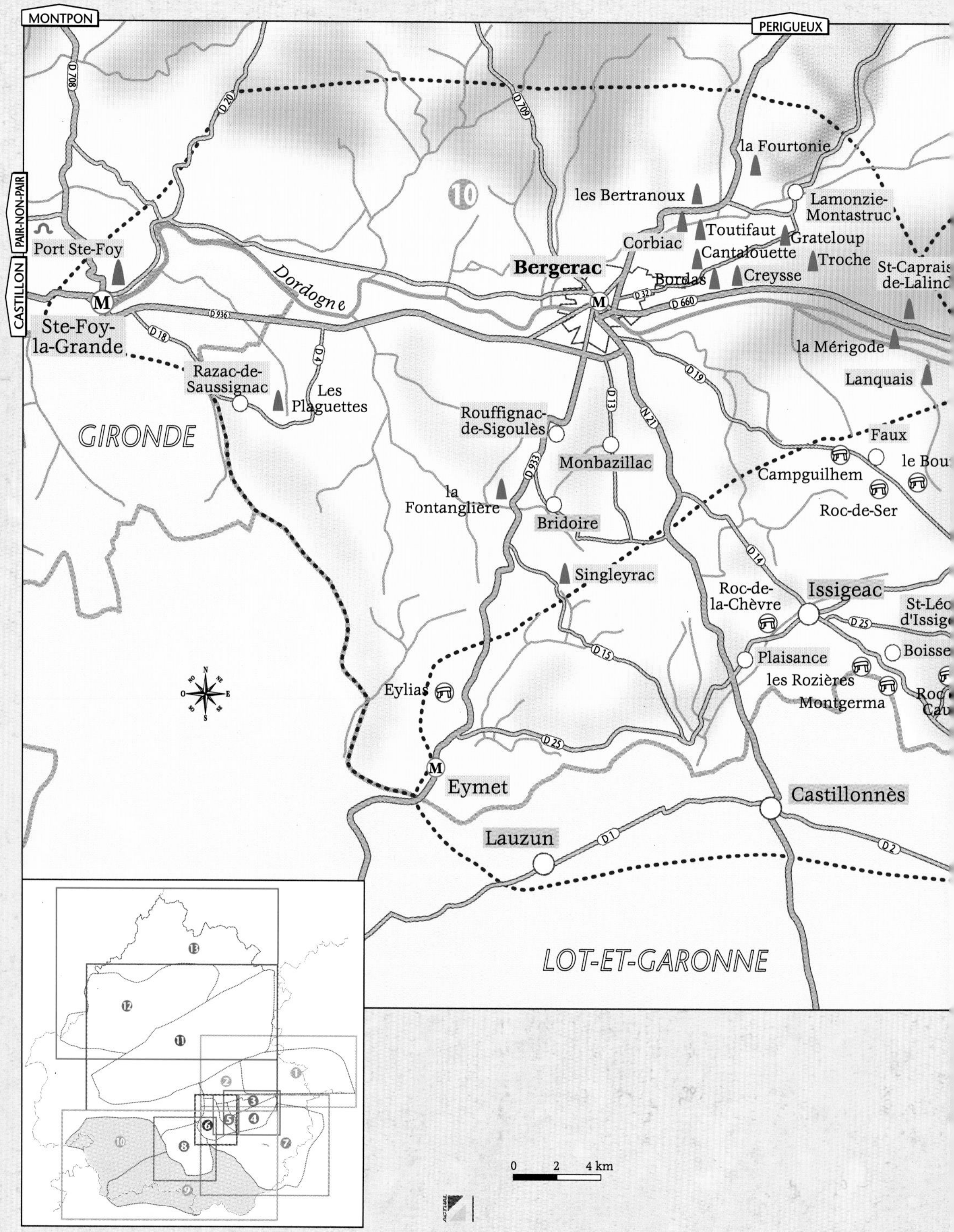

MONTPON
PERIGUEUX
PAIR-NON-PAIR
CASTILLON
D 708
D 20
D 709
10
la Fourtonie
les Bertranoux
Lamonzie-Montastruc
Toutifaut
Grateloup
Corbiac
Cantalouette
Troche
Port Ste-Foy
Bergerac
Bordas
Creysse
St-Caprais-de-Lalind
Dordogne
D 32
D 660
M
Ste-Foy-la-Grande
D 936
D 18
D 4
la Mérigode
Razac-de-Saussignac
Les Plaguettes
Lanquais
D 19
D 13
Rouffignac-de-Sigoulès
GIRONDE
Faux
Monbazillac
N 21
le Bou
Campguilhem
la Fontanglière
D 933
Roc-de-Ser
Bridoire
D 14
Singleyrac
Roc-de-la-Chèvre
Issigeac
St-Léo d'Issig
D 25
D 15
Plaisance
Boisse
les Rozières
Eylias
Montgerma
D 25
Eymet
Castillonnès
Lauzun
D 1
D 2
LOT-ET-GARONNE
13
12
11
2
1
3
5
4
6
10
8
7
9
0 2 4 km

# From Belvès to Bergerac

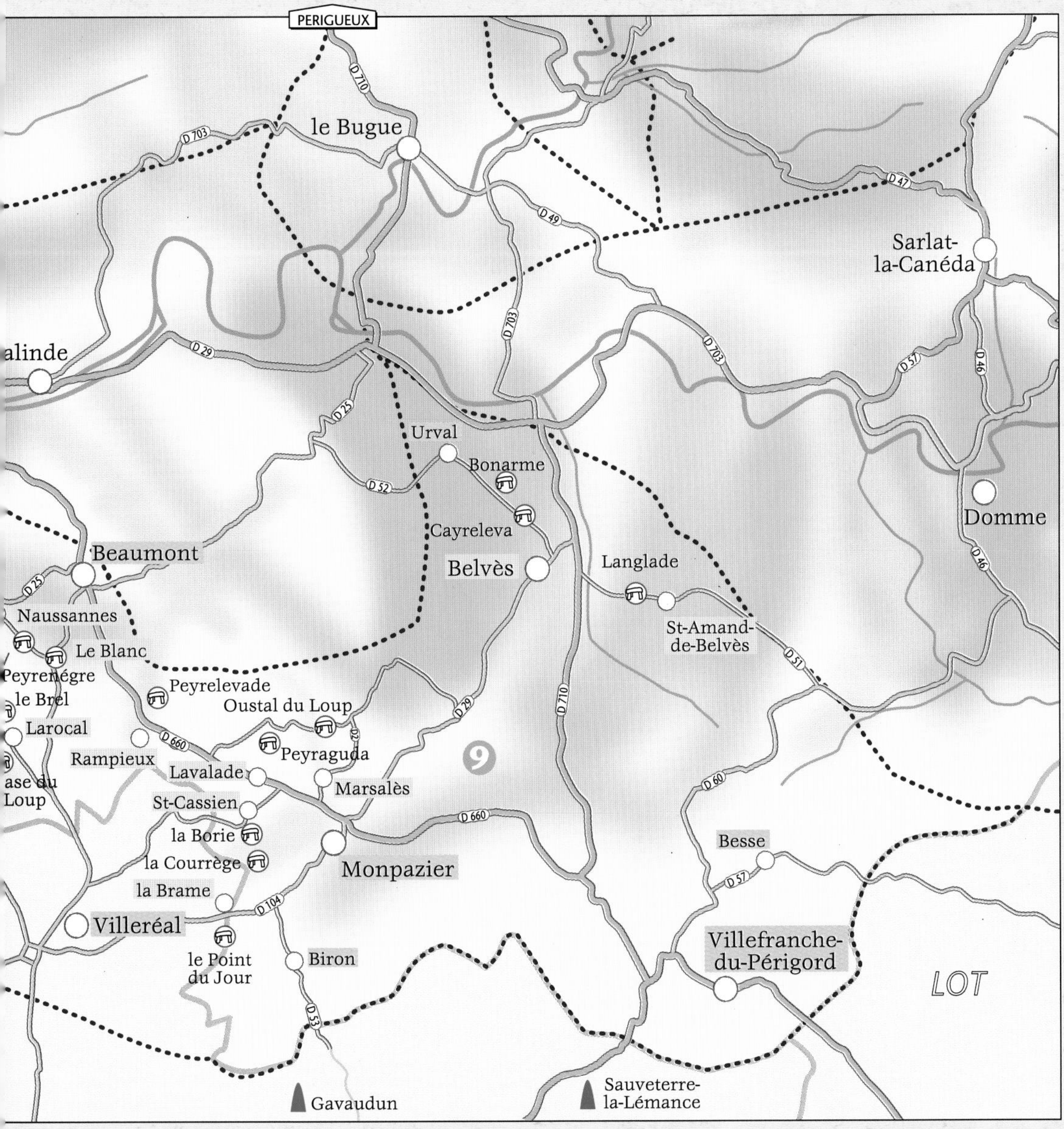

PERIGUEUX
D 710
D 703
le Bugue
D 47
D 49
Sarlat-
la-Canéda
D 703
D 29
alinde
D 703
D 57
D 46
D 25
Urval
Bonarme
D 52
Domme
Cayreleva
Beaumont
Belvès
Langlade
D 46
D 25
Naussannes
St-Amand-
de-Belvès
Le Blanc
D 51
Peyrenégre
Peyrelevade
le Brel
Oustal du Loup
D 29
D 710
Larocal
D 660
Peyraguda
Rampieux
9
ase du
Loup
Lavalade
Marsalès
D 60
St-Cassien
D 660
la Borie
Besse
la Courrège
Monpazier
la Brame
D 57
D 104
Villeréal
Villefranche-
du-Périgord
le Point
du Jour
Biron
LOT
D 53
Gavaudun
Sauveterre-
la-Lémance

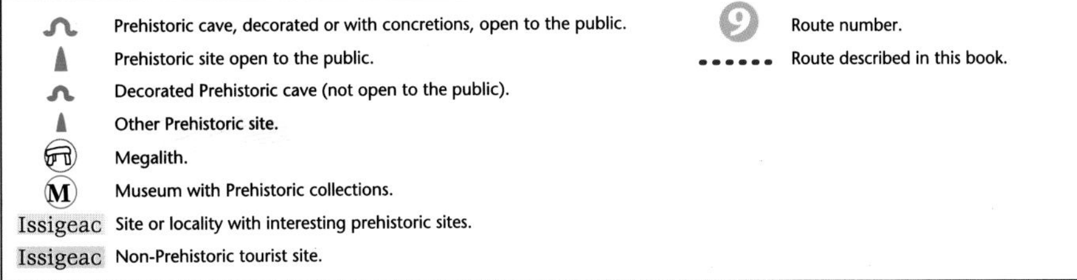

## Sites open to visitors between Belvès and Eymet

***Eymet*** *museum*
***Le Blanc*** *dolmen, at* ***Nojals-et-Clottes***
***Beaumont*** *Tourist Bureau, tel. 05.53.22.39.12.*
***Belvès*** *Tourist Bureau, tel. 05.53.29.10.20.*
***Eymet*** *Tourist Bureau, tel. 05.53.23.74.95.*
***Issigeac*** *Tourist Bureau, tel. 05.53.58.79.62.*
***Monpazier*** *Tourist Bureau, tel. 05.53.22.68.59.*
***Villefranche-du-Périgord*** *Tourist Bureau, tel. 05.53.29.98.37.*

*Most dolmens are left "in their natural state", in the middle of woods or the corner of a field. They can be visited, as long as private property is respected and crops are not damaged. The GR 36 leads walkers from Saint-Cyprien to Belvès, and then to Monpazier.*

*Apart from prehistoric curiosities, the traveller must not miss the medieval cities of Belvès and Issigeac, the bastides (fortified towns) of Villefranche-du-Périgord, Monpazier, Beaumont, Eymet, Monflanquin, Villeréal, Castillonnès, the Biron and Bonagil castles, and the churches of Urval and Besse.*

## Sites open to visitors in Bergeracois and Bordelais country

***Bergerac*** *museum (Maison Peyrarède), tel. 05.53.63.04.13.*
***Sainte-Foy-la-Grande*** *museum*
*Aquitaine museum, at* ***Bordeaux****, tel. 05.56.01.51.00.*
***Pair-Non-Pair*** *cave, at* ***Prignac-et-Marcamps****, tel. 05.57.68.33.40.*
***Bergerac*** *Tourist Office, tel. 05.53.57.03.11.*
***Sainte-Foy-la-Grande*** *Tourist Office, tel. 05.57.46.03.00.*
***Bordeaux*** *Tourist Office, tel. 05.56.00.66.00.*
***Sainte-Alvère*** *Tourist Bureau, tel. 05.53.27.59.99.*
***Saussignac*** *Tourist Bureau, tel. 05.53.22.49.11.*
***Sigoulès*** *Tourist Bureau, tel. 05.53.58.48.16.*
***Vergt*** *Tourist Bureau, tel. 05.53.03.45.10.*
***Villefranche-de-Lonchat*** *Tourist Bureau, tel. 05.53.58.63.16.*

*The GR 6 follows the left bank of the river Dordogne, past Lalinde, Couze, Lanquais and Montbazillac. Do not miss the old town of Bergerac, the vineyards and châteaux of Montbazillac, Lanquais and Montaigne, which are open to visitors.*

*Near Beaumont, the Le Blanc gallery tomb: 5,000 to 7,000 years old.*

## BETWEEN BELVÈS AND ISSIGEAC: THE DOLMENS OF BASTIDES COUNTRY

Route 9

### Around Belvès

Brittany is not the only place to have dolmens. The old prehistoric territory of Périgord has about 200 megaliths, and many more were destroyed over the centuries. Over 6,000 years after the artists of the reindeer age disappeared, that is 4,000 to 2,000 B.C., Neolithic men of the Copper Age covered our country with stone monuments. South of the Dordogne river, "bastide country" holds many of them, amongst the finest.

In the commune of Siorac, following the road from Belvès to Urval, after Bonarme, the Cayreleva dolmen is signposted on the right. A kilometre (half a mile) further on, in a garden, there is a fine stone table, 1.5 metres high (5 ft.), under which polished stone axes were found. Two hundred metres (220 yds) from Bonarme (in the commune of Saint-Pardoux-et-Vielvic), on a path, there is a sign to the "Bonne-Arme dolmen". Half buried under a tumulus, this dolmen has three cupules, carved out according to legend by the hoofs of a cow or the Devil's horse. A few kilometres further on, near the Saint-Amand-de-Belvès town hall, at the edge of the road in private property, one can see the fine Langlade dolmen, more than 3 metres long (10 ft.), and surrounded by blocks of stone which could be menhirs. Above Urval, the unfinished bastide of Castelréal protects a Bronze Age site.

### Between Beaumont and Monpazier: the Le Blanc gallery tomb

The next stop is three kilometres (2 miles) south of the Beaumont bastide, next to the D 676, (commune of Nojals-et-Clottes) one of the most beautiful megaliths in Périgord: the Le Blanc gallery tomb. Two tables and seven supports are still in place, the whole ensemble

### *Neolithic*

*The Neolithic era, or age of polished stone, extends from 5,000 to 2,000 B.C. The "agricultural revolution", which had already taken place in the Middle East, reached Périgord about 5,000 B.C. Together with agriculture and stock-breeding, tools, morals and beliefs were greatly modified. Trees had to be cut down, and grain stored. Between 5,000 and 2,000 B.C., many dolmens were erected on Perigordian territory. There still remain more than 200, especially in the south of the département. These artificial caves served as tombs. Later around 2,000 B.C., collective sepulchral caves were used, such as that at Campniac, near Périgueux, or Eybral in the Dordogne valley.*

measuring more than 12 metres (40 ft.). According to legend, the Virgin Mary set these stones to protect a shepherdess caught in a storm... or by some rascal. A little further on, next to the Naussanes road, one finds the Peyre-Nègre dolmen, 2 metres high (6.5 ft.).

To the south, one can visit the two megaliths of Sainte-Sabine. On the D 24, at Larocal, entering the woods, the huge Case du Loup dolmen rises up to a height of 2.5 metres (8 ft.), and is 3 metres long (10 ft.). But be careful! Legend says that a giant wolf, a monster with flaming eyes, sometimes comes there. Further on, 500 metres (550 yds) from Pincanelle, the Roc de Cause dolmen is 5 metres long (16 ft.). At Rampieux, Peyrelevade, in the middle of a field, there is a dolmen settled peacefully under a tumulus. At Saint-Cassien, on the Tourliac road, at La Borie, Neolithic man left a huge stone polisher. After the village of Barriat, direction La Courrège, next to a path, one finds a second gallery tomb 6 metres long (20 ft.), with thirteen supports remaining. A hundred metres (110 yds) from the D 2, in the commune of Marsalès, at La Borie-Neuve, there is a third gallery tomb, Oustal-du-Loup. It still has thirteen pillars, for 7 metres in length (23 ft.).

Four kilometres (2.5 miles) from the Monpazier bastide, at Lavalade, stands the Peyraguda menhir. At the edge of Lot-et-Garonne, next to the D 104, near the La Brame hamlet (Vergt-de-Biron hamlet), the Point-du-Jour dolmen is one of the biggest in Périgord, 6 metres long (about 20 ft.).

*The Le Blanc gallery tomb, one of the finest megaliths of Périgord.*

### A step into Lot-et-Garonne, between Fumel and Gavaudun: the Sauveterrian period

In 1928, the discovery of the Martinet shelter, at Sauveterre-la-Lémance in Lot-et-Garonne, defined the Sauveterrian period (8,000 B.C.). Characteristic of this Mesolithic period are the tiny chipped flints used as arrow tips. Near Fumel, the Monsempron and Las Pelenos caves, and the Pronquière cave at Saint-Georges, are Mousterian. Right next to the Périgord border, south of Biron, Gavaudun possesses three sites extending from the Mousterian to the Perigordian: Plateau-Baillard, Peyrony and Roc-de-Gavaudun. At Trentels, the Cassegros cave (Magdalenian) is the only decorated cave in the *département.*

### From Issigeac to Eymet: a wandering English general

Further west, the Issigeac region is also rich in megaliths. Apart from the Rozières dolmen, Boisse possesses a menhir, at the edge of the road, at Mongerma. In a field at Le Brel, in the commune of Saint-Léon-d'Issigeac, one can find a dolmen which is almost square, 4 metres (13 ft.) on each side. At Fondargent, near Plaisance, the Roc de la Chèvre (Goat Rock) is said to guard the body of an English general killed during the Hundred Years' War. At Faux, a path leads to the Campguilhem dolmen, which is also said to cover the remains of an Englishman, Captain Guilhem, killed in action. Right by the D 19, at Le Bourdil, the Pierre du Général (General's Stone), also guards the "wandering skeleton" of an English officer. At least four dolmens in Périgord claim the glory of serving as sepulchre to the invader. In fact, at Le Bourdil, skulls, bones and arrow tips were found, but from long before the Hundred Years' War. In Les Grèses, also next to the D 19, there is a huge flat stone 5 metres long (16 ft.), all that remains of the Roc de Ser dolmen. If one says an *Ave Maria* there, the stone will turn around nine times. Try, and you will see! To the very south of the *département*, about one kilometre (half a mile) from the bastide, or fortified town, of Eymet, at Eylias, there is a classical dolmen, on four supports, hidden among the vines. The Eymet museum has some interesting prehistoric collections on display.

## AROUND BERGERAC, IN PÉRIGORD POURPRE

Route ⑩

### Lanquais, the Ruhr of silex

After Couze, the landscape changes, the cliffs are rarer and only on the right bank of the Dordogne, the prehistoric sites are found at the bottom of the valleys, the middle terraces of the river, on stepped shoulders on the slopes, the slopes themselves, the tops of the plateaux, and in the fields. For, contrary to what had been thought, man did not simply stay sheltering under rocks, even when the climate was harsh. Between Lalinde and Sainte-Foy-la-Grande, more than 100 sites have been excavated and nearly 300 catalogued. This region was highly populated because of the wealth of a top quality raw material, found in enormous kidney shapes (sometimes as big as a man's thigh): silex. The region can be called a "Ruhr of silex". And it was literally "exported" to other regions which were less well endowed. But since they were covered with a thin sedimentary layer, many of these deposits were destroyed by agriculture and civil engineering. They were also the prey of many collectors. Before 1914, the baker at Cours-de-Pile, who specialized in this sort of trade, sold Abbé Breuil his first collection, after a seminar. Since they had been "skimmed", amputated of their remains of bones (destroyed by the acidity of the soil), these sites were considered to be of no interest for scientific research until recently. But systematic prospecting and excavation, between 1957 and 1971 (J. and G. Guichard), discovered a whole series of deposits perfectly in place, certain of them stratigraphic, and revealed "structures" rich in information.

Leaving Couze, several kilometres to the south-west, one discovers Lanquais (do not miss the château) and its forest, where each tree uprooted discloses hundreds of products from stone sawing (Campignian). One is standing on a gigantic workshop for carving axes, picks, paring knives, and land-clearing tools. One is at the dawn of agriculture (locally this took place around 2,000 to 1,500 B.C.), which implied clearing the thick forest (particularly Norway pine, excavations by M.-C. Cauvin, 1965). This series of workshops close to each

***Striker and box-wood hammer used for chipping flints.***

other extends over several dozens of acres: La Mérigode is the biggest. This same industry, in the same proportions, can be found at Les Platans (Saint-Capraise-de-Lalinde) and at La Canéda-Fourtonie (Lamonzie-Montastruc).

Near Lanquais, the Rabier Palaeolithic site (Upper Perigordian to microgravettian) occupies the bottom of the little valley of the Caudeau. It is very rich (with several tens of thousands of objects over about 200 square metres, or 240 sq. yds, scraping horizontally), and contains among other things an engraving, traces of painting, and especially the biggest palaeolithic blades known (up to 35 centimetres, or 14 inches), which were only exceeded in the Magdalenian period in "hut" structures (discovery and excavation J. and G. Guichard, 1961, now in the Les Eyzies museum).

## Bergerac, Prehistory among the vines

Between Mouleydier and Bergerac, and especially around Creysse, capital of Pécharmant, on the right bank of the river, there is a multitude of sites spanning the Acheulian and Magdalenian periods: Cantalouette (Acheulian); Les Pendus (Middle Acheulian, around 200,000 B.C.) which produced more than 300 bifaces of a special type in less than 20 square metres, or 24 sq. yds (Les Pendus type); the Bertrannoux (Upper Acheulian); the Barbas site (several layers of Acheulian and Mousterian of Acheulian tradition, topped by a layer of Aurignacian). There again, a few square metres held 6 to 20 bifaces. Very close by, the Troche and Canaule I sites contained evidence of this industry which was unknown until then: from the technical point of view, it is like a "passage" between the Middle Palaeolithic and Upper Palaeolithic. Canaule II, with its structures, is Châtelperronian, and the "Henri Factory", above Canaule, is from the final Magdalenian period (all discovered and excavated by J. and G. Guichard, and now in the Les Eyzies museum).

Three kilometres (2 miles) from Bergerac, in the very rich deposits of the Corbiac château, (excavations F. Bordes), there was an extensive Gravettian industry, from the Upper Perigordian. It gave its name to a type of burin.

A little to the north-west, near Maurens, there are other sites such as Aillas (sometimes called Aillac), a Perigordian habitat similar to Corbiac, and Toutifaut, where Mousterian objects of Acheulian tradition and Aurignacian objects are present in unbelievable numbers (excavations J. and G. Guichard, in the Les Eyzies museum). There are many other sites which are less important or have been more damaged, which need not be mentioned here. However, there is Grateloup near the château of the philosopher Maine de Biran. Evidently, there are Neolithic remains everywhere, but since they were more superficial, they have been completely dispersed or collected, and the fine polished axes are impossible to find. The very beautiful site of Fontanglière, at Rouffignac-de-Sigoulès, is an especially regrettable example, since a splendid Chalcolithic sepulchral cave with many skeletons and a wealth of objects (including superb flint daggers) was completely pillaged and all the remains dispersed.

Some fine examples of all these industries can be seen in the Bergerac Museum of Prehistory, in the old part of the town which has been renovated, next to the Museum of Sacred Art, the River Transport Museum and the Tobacco Museum, all well worth a visit.

At Razac-de-Saussignac, the Plaguettes site produced a terracotta figurine dating from the Artenacian (4,000 B.C.). At Port-Sainte-Foy and at Fleix, the river Dordogne hid bronze weapons, discovered when dredging.

It is worthwhile visiting the Sainte-Foy-la-Grande museum, the land of Broca, founder of physical anthropology (who studied the skulls of Cro-Magnon man), of Elisée Reclus the great geographer, and of Elie Faure, a fine historian of French art. It is a high point of the wealth of Périgord: at the gates of Gironde...

## Following the Dordogne, from Sainte-Foy to Bordeaux: the Pair-Non-Pair cave

In Gironde, the banks of the Dordogne are layered with important prehistoric sites. At Pessac-sur-Dordogne, the Morin shelter revealed a rich supply of Magdalenian portable art. At Lugasson, the Mitrot cave holds a tectiform, probably Magdalenian, just like its neighbouring Fontarnaud cave. At Cessac, the Faustin shelter contains Magdalenian engravings, as does the Pille-Bourse shelter, at Saint-Germain-la-Rivière (a horse and a human figure). At Saint-Quentin-de-Baron there are two Magdalenian sites: Moulin-Neuf and the Jaurias cave, and the Lespaux Gravettian shelter. At Marcamps, the Pair-Non-Pair (Even-Uneven) decorated cave, discovered in 1881, and frequented from Mousterian to Perigordian times, has revealed Aurignacian works of art. It is considered to be the oldest decorated cave in the world. The public can visit it, to admire its seven panels engraved with prehistoric animals. In the same commune, one can also see the Fées cave, surmounted by the Roc-de-Marcamps deposit, both Magdalenian.

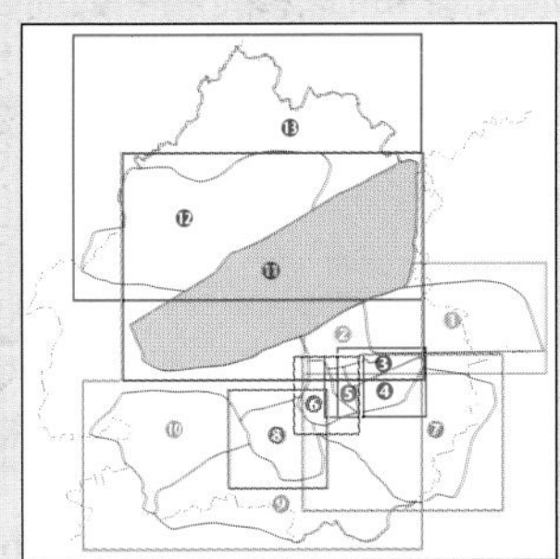

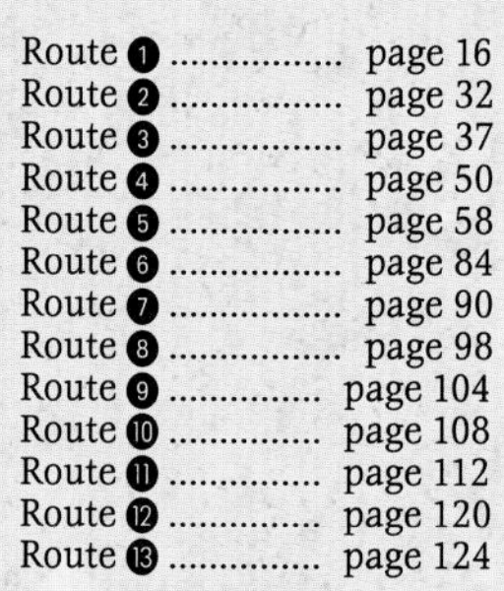


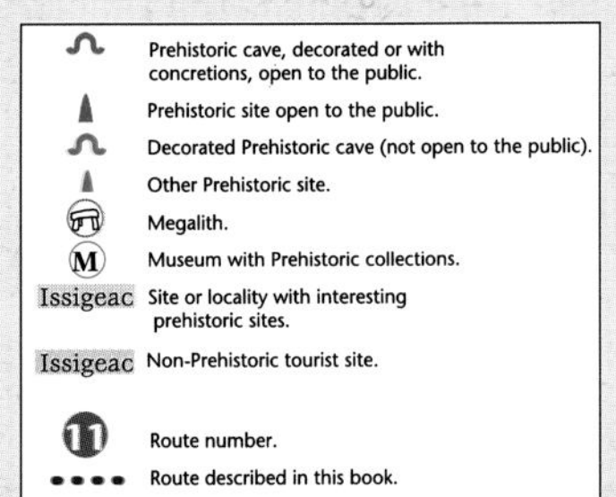

NONTRON
Mareuil
D 939
D 708
D 675
Dronne
D 702
Brantôme
D 78
D 709
D 939
la Pelletenie
Agonac
Jaillac
D 20
Ribérac
D 710
D 5
Merlande
Raymonden
D 708
D 709
Chancelade
le Toulon
les Bori
M
PERIGUEUX
N 2089
Campniac
St-Astier
N 89
D 3
Fontaine des Demoiselles
St-Léon-sur-l'Isle
Neuvic
N 89
Solvieux
Grignols
St-Louis
Isle
Fratteau
St-Front-de-Pradoux
Plateau Parrain
Gâbillou
D 3
N 89
Mussidan
N 21
D 8
MONTPON
Mont-Réal
D 38
112
D 709
D 20
BERGERAC

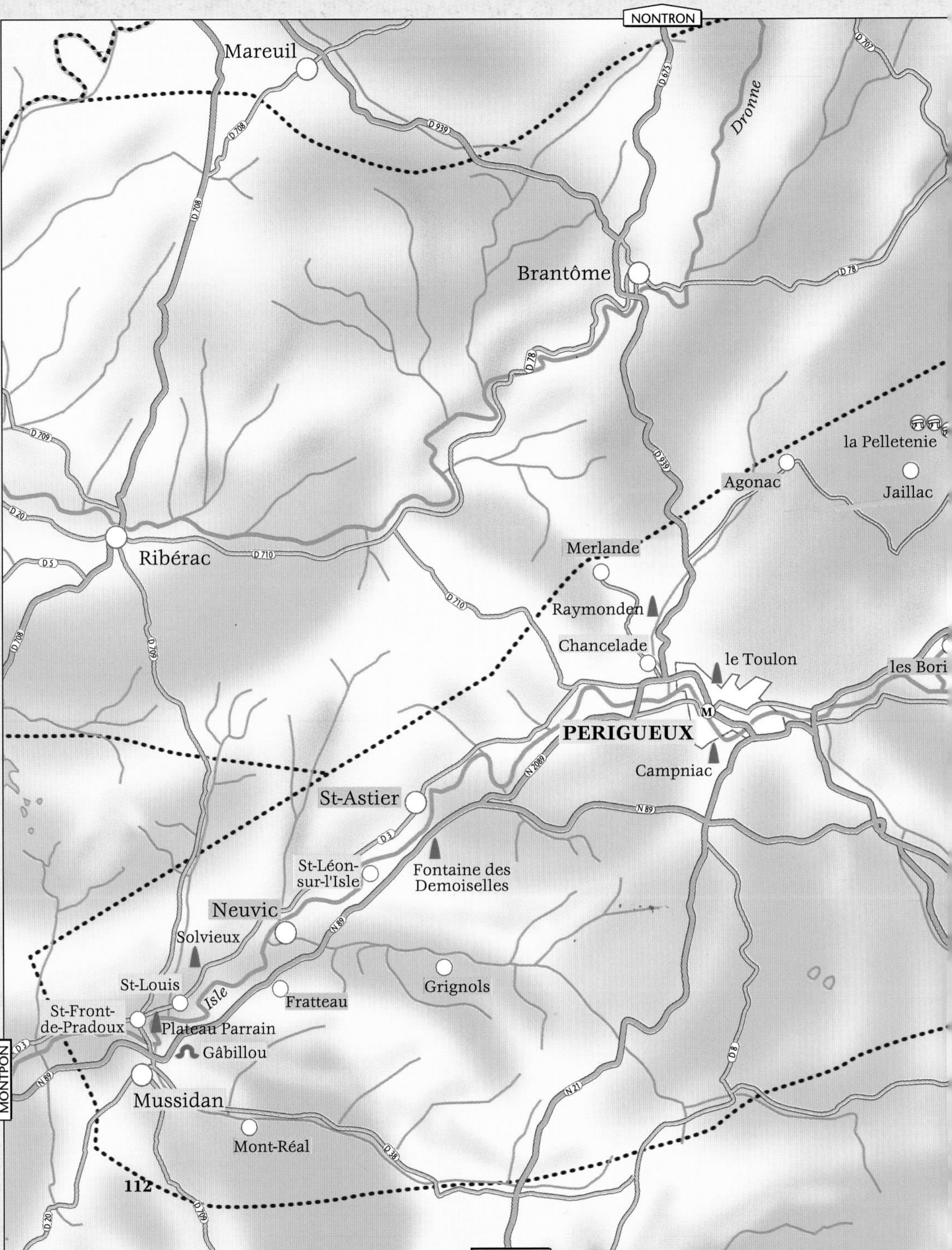

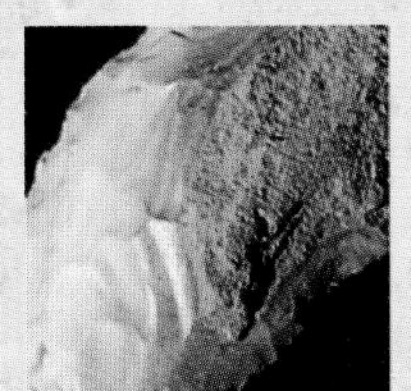

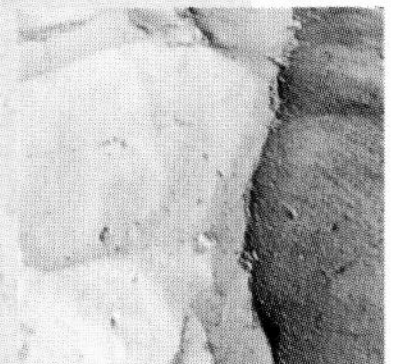

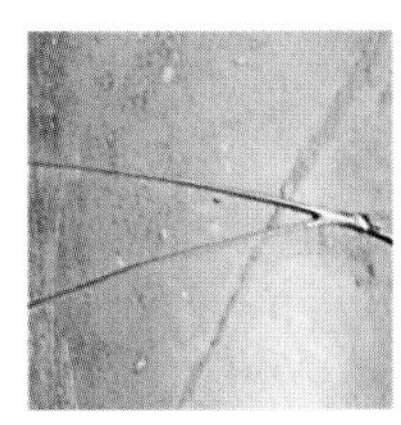

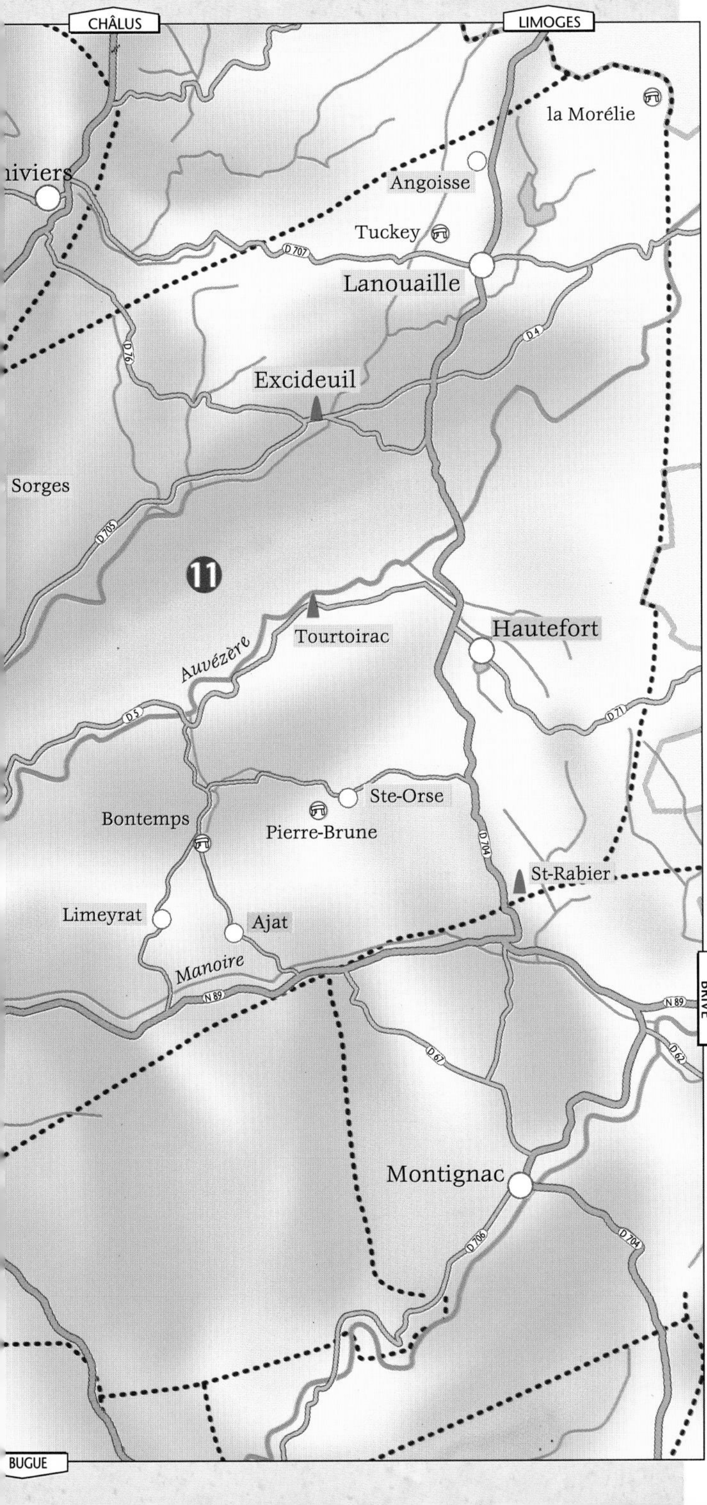

# Around Périgueux

## *Sites open to visitors in the Isle Valley*

*Perigord Museum, at* ***Périgueux****, tel. 05.53.53.16.42.*

*Départemental Tourist Office, tel. 05.53.53.44.35.*

***Périgueux*** *Tourist Office, tel. 05.53.53.10.63.*
***Excideuil*** *Tourist Bureau, tel. 05.53.62.95.56.*
***Hautefort*** *Tourist Bureau, tel. 05.53.50.40.27.*
***Lanouaille*** *Tourist Bureau, tel. 05.53.62.17.82.*
***Montpon*** *Tourist Bureau, tel. 05.53.82.23.73.*
***Mussidan*** *Tourist Bureau, tel. 05.53.81.04.77.*
***Saint-Astier*** *Tourist Bureau, tel. 05.53.54.13.85.*
***Saint-Aulaye*** *Tourist Bureau, tel. 05.53.90.63.74.*
***Sorges*** *Tourist Bureau, tel. 05.53.05.90.11.*

*Walkers can follow the Isle valley, from Périgueux to Mussidan, taking the GR 646, and can explore the Chancelade area with the GR 36. Even though the prehistoric sites of the Isle valley are not open to the public, visitors can compensate for this by seeing the many châteaux (Hautefort, Les Bories, Neuvic, Frateau, Montréal), churches and abbeys (Tourtoirac, Chancelade, Merlande, Saint-Astier), the* ***old town of Périgueux*** *and the Truffle Ecomuseum at Sorges.*

## PÉRIGUEUX AND THE ISLE VALLEY

Route ⓫

### Around Excideuil: the Auvézère and the upper valley of the Isle

The Isle, a tributary of the Dordogne, which crosses the middle of the *département* from east to west, has few noteworthy prehistoric sites. To the east, watered by the Loue, a tributary of the Isle, Angoisse hides a little dolmen under a tumulus, at La Morélie. In Lanouaille, the Tuckey tumulus has provided a recipient and an ear-ring from the Iron Age (800 B.C.). Downstream, near Excideuil; the Eglise cave, excavated as early as 1869, held ornaments and a child's skeleton in its Solutrean and Magdalenian levels. The small Tourtoirac cave, on the Auvézère, the main tributary of the Isle, was inhabited in the Aurignacian period, the Upper Perigordian and the Solutrean. Very near, at Les Ourteix, an open-air Mousterian prehistoric site was found in 1972. On the slopes, south of the Auvézère, one finds the Bontemps dolmen at Limeyrat and, at Sainte-Orse, the Pierre-Brune megalith which is locally believed to be a meteor. At Saint-Rabier, the Peyrat site revealed an Azilian tomb containing the skeletons of a man and a woman. On the right bank of the Isle, Sorges guards three megaliths, near La Pelletinie: the Sorges dolmen, the La Pelletinie dolmen, strangely made of two tables in an inversed V, and the Clapier megalith near the D 8.

***Opposite page:* *An urn with a foot, with graphitized decor characteristic of the first Iron Age in eastern Périgord.***
**Périgord Museum at Périgueux.**
Photo B. Dupuy.

***A bracelet from the middle Bronze Age, discovered in the Calévie cave at Meyrals.*** **Périgord Museum at Périgueux**
Photo B. Dupuy.

*chipped flints: Levalloisian nucleus (top left), convex scraper (top right), point (bottom right). Small amulet axe, arrow head, scraper (bottom left), Neolithic.* **Périgord Museum, Périgueux.**

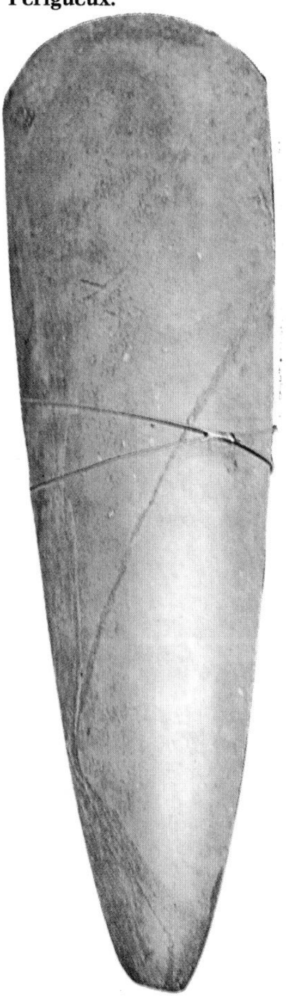

*Polished axe, Neolithic.* **Périgord Museum, Périgueux.**

## Périgueux and Chancelade

In Périgueux, one must not miss visiting the Périgord museum (allées Tourny) since its prehistoric collections are so rich, before going on to a high-point of Prehistory: Chancelade.

Apart from the Chancelade and "Chez Pigeassou" shelters, the Raymonden cave, not far from the abbey, is one of Périgord's most important prehistoric sites. In fact, under two shelters, it is the only one to hold the complete stratigraphy of the Magdalenian era (from 15,000 to 9,000 B.C.). In 1888, Féaux and Hardy discovered the skeleton of "Chancelade man", a contemporary of Cro-Magnon man, but shorter (1.55 metres or 5ft. 1in.) and of "eskimo" type. One can imagine the cultural wealth of Chancelade man from the many lithic and bone industries there, ornaments (teeth, shells, pendants) and portable art (bone engraving industry).

On the heights of Périgueux, at Coulounieix-Chamiers, the Campniac cave contained human bones, polished axes, pottery and ornaments dating from the Middle and Upper Neolithic (around 3,000 B.C.). The neighbouring hill of Ecornebœuf was still densely populated at the time of the Gauls. A lance tip and a pin dating from the end of the Bronze Age were found at Toulon.

## Mussidan-le-Gabillou and the lower Isle valley

Downstream, one kilometre (half a mile) east of Mussidan, at Sourzac, the Gabillou engraved cave is one of the most important in the whole of France. It is the only decorated cave in the Isle valley, but unfortunately it is not open to the public because its walls are very fragile. It holds about 200 engravings, from the early Magdalenian era, which means they can be compared with those of Lascaux. The themes are the usual ones: horses, auroch, bison, reindeer, ibex and felines. However, one can see two hares and two interesting human representations: a man with a bison's head and tail, the "Gabillou sorcerer", and a woman wearing a sort of anorak with a hood. The cave was discovered in 1941, and studied by the most eminent prehistorians, including Breuil, Peyrony, Leroi-Gourhan and J. Gaussen. Its decoration is sometimes surprising: hares, dogs, cats, birds and weasels are in fact very rare subjects in palaeolithic art. The open-air deposit of Tares, close to Gabillou but remote in time, discovered in 1972, was inhabited by Neanderthal man. His Mousterian tooling is mainly of the Quina type.

And there is yet more Prehistory in Mussidan. Apart from the sites of Dauby, Saint-Georges, La Forge and the Chatenades, there is the open-air settlement of Plateau-Parrain, on the banks of the Isle, inhabited in the Middle Magdalenian. J.Gaussen found the base of a tent there, 4 metres (13 ft.) by 4.5 metres (15 ft), and made up of pebbles. At Saint-Louis-en-Isle, close by, the open-air site of Solvieux extends over 3 hectares (7.5 acres). There are traces from the Aurignacian, Perigordian and Magdalenian periods there. Vast stretches of paving, as at Plateau-Parrain, are evidence of a camp from the Middle Magdalenian, a type of habitat which seems to be specific to the Isle valley. At Saint-Léon-sur-l'Isle, the Fontaine de la Demoiselle is a fortified camp dating back to the recent Neolithic.

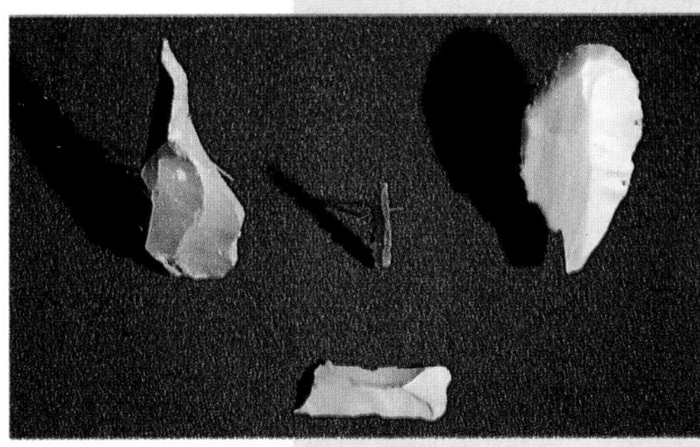

***Scrapers and other domestic objects.* Périgord Museum, Périgueux.**

***Discovered near the Toulon Hermitage at Perigueux, a spear head in bronze, decorated.* Périgord Museum, Périgueux.** Photo B. Dupuy.

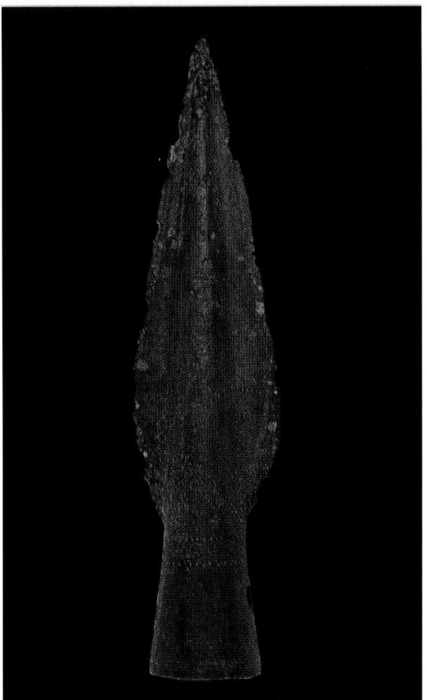

### *Copper, Bronze and Iron, the apparance of metal*

*Copper first appeared in Périgord around 3,000 B.C. (Chalcolithic sepulchral cave of La Fontanguillère containing copper daggers). About 2,000 B.C. bronze was discovered, an alloy of copper and tin. Trade exchanges multiplied, to obtain these precious materials. In Périgord, there are many remains from this epoch: the sepulchral cave of the Partisans at Marquay, bracelets from Calévie, at Meyrals, the Singleyrac treasure, swords from Saint-Paul-Lizonne and Port-Sainte-Foy, a dagger from Coux, the Toulon tip of a lance, at Périgueux, deposits of axes in Fleurac, Thonac and Vanxains, the habitats of Le Roque-Saint-Christophe, Rouffignac and Vauffrey. Iron began to replace bronze only after 800 B.C. Since Périgord was rich in iron ores, it became wealthy. Remains from this epoch can be found at the Ecornebœuf habitat, on the heights of Périgueux and the burial tumuli of Lanouaille and Jumilhac-le-Grand.*

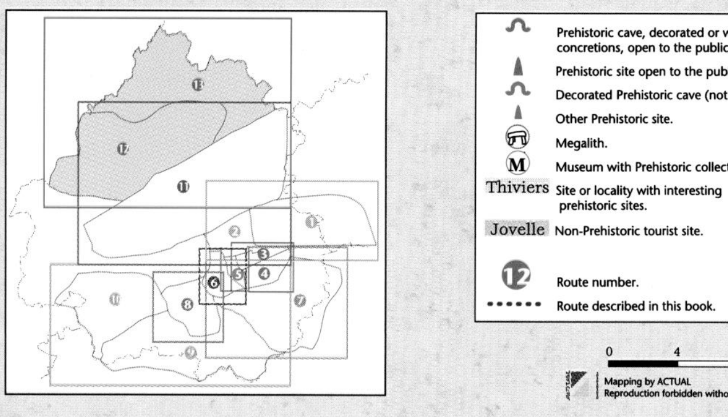


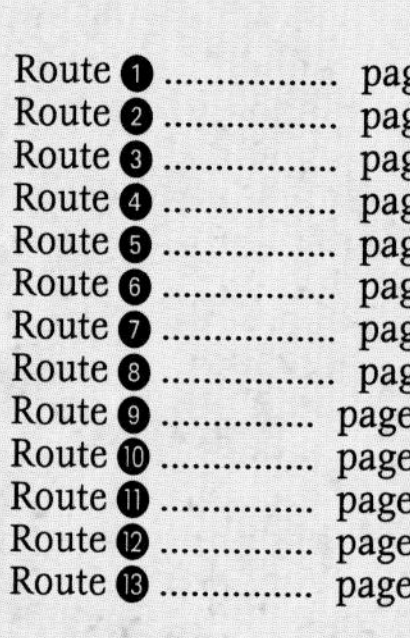


ANGOULÊME
Fontechevade
Bussière-Badil
la Chaise
Grotte du Quéroy
le Placard
Montgau-dier
la Pierre Plate
Fixard
Piégut
Roc de Sers
Varaignes
St-Estèphe (Roc Branlant)
Teyjat
CHARENTE
Bandiat
la Chaire à Calvin
Nontron
La Quina
Champeaux
St-Sulpice-de-Mareuil
Font-Bargeix
la Rochebeaucourt
Bernardières
Puyrignac
Mareuil
Vieux-Mareuil
Dronne
Fronsac
Richemont
Puyguilhem
Boschaud
Cherval
12
le Breuil
Paussac-et-St-Vivien
Brantôme
le Fouret
Jovelle
le Fourneau du Diable
Chapelle-Fauc
la Pierre Levée
St-Paul-Lizonne
Peyre Dermale
les Bernous
les Rebières
Peyrelevade
Fonseigner
Grand-Brassac
Jambe-Grosse
Allemans
Beauroulet
Aubeterre-sur-Dronne
Celles
Rochereil
Valeuil
Bourdeilles
Ribérac
Tocane-St-Apre
Pont d'Ambon
la Bourgeade
St-Privat
St-Martin
Festalemps
la Vaurélie
Vanxains
Margot
PERIGUEUX
Sauteranne
Seyssac
St-Aquilin
St-Aulaye
Siorac-de-Ribérac
St-Astier
MONTPON
LE BUG
D 90
D 91
D 939
D 674
D 675
D 75
D 708
D 84
D 98
D 93
D 78
D 10
D 709
D 20
D 710
D 5
D 3
N 2089
N 89

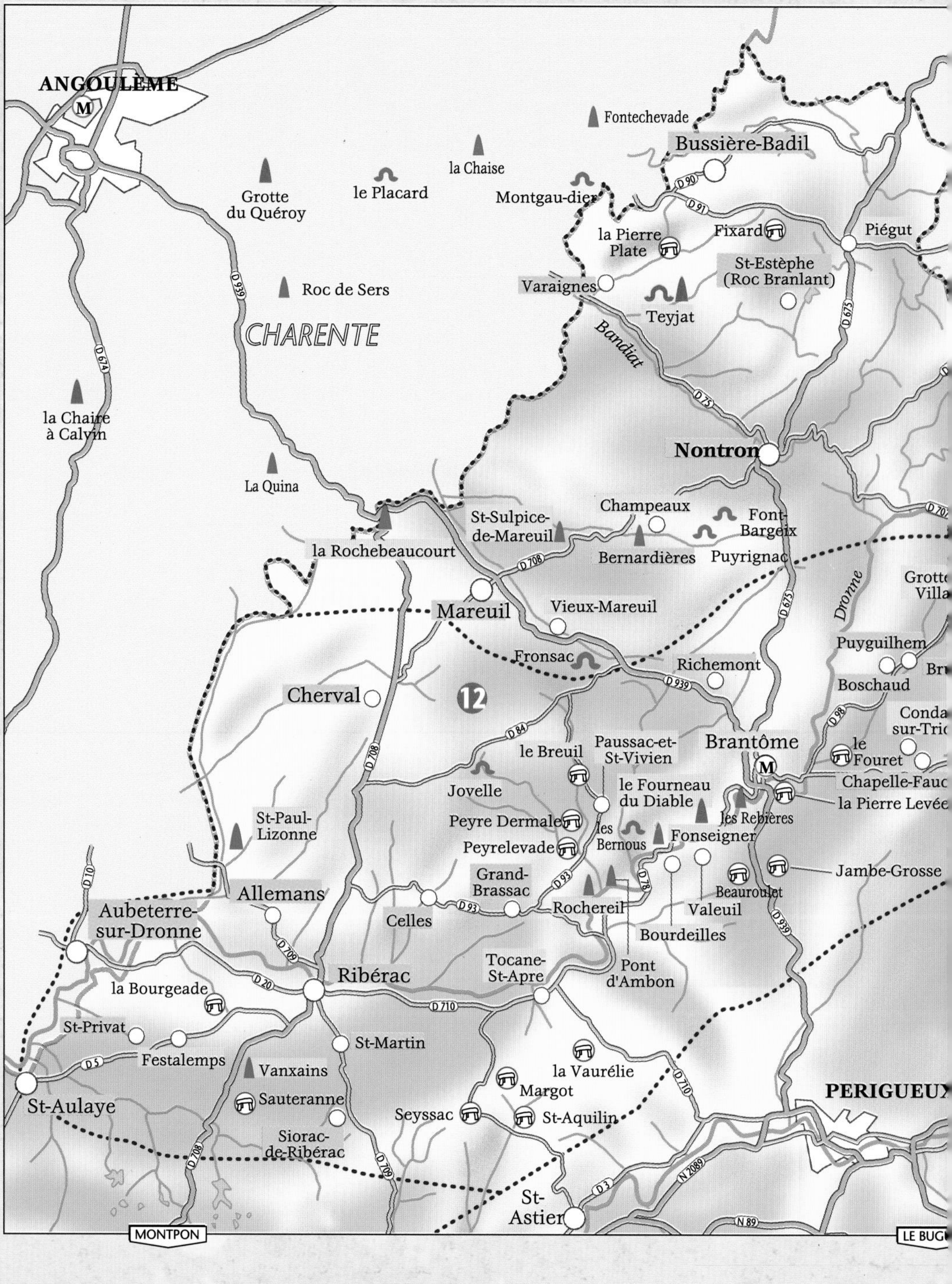

# North Périgord

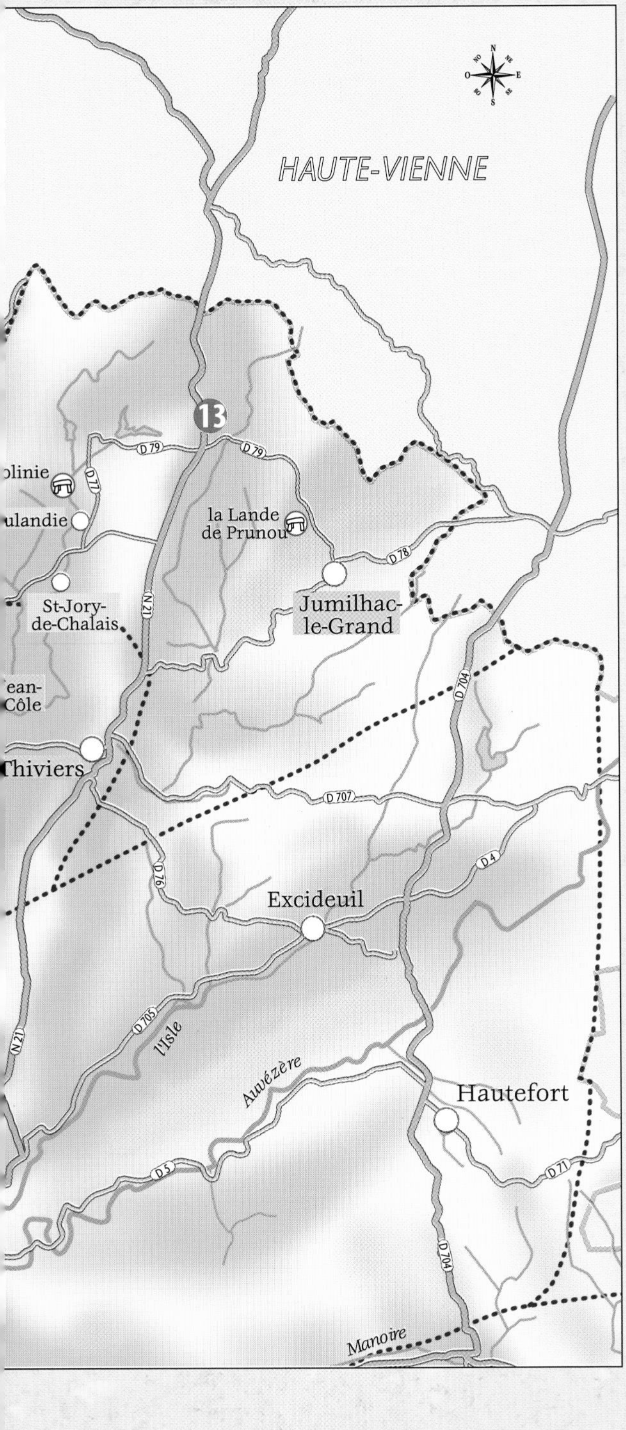

## Sites open to visitors in the Dronne valley

***Villars*** *cave, tel. 05.53.54.82.36.*
***Le Fourneau du Diable*** *site*
***Brantôme*** *museum*

***Ribérac*** *Tourist Office, tel. 05.53.90.03.10.*
***Brantôme*** *Tourist Bureau, tel. 05.53.05.80.52.*
***Bordeilles*** *Tourist Bureau, tel. 05.53.03.42.96.*
***Villars*** *Tourist Bureau, tel. 05.53.62.14.15.*
***La Coquille*** *Tourist Bureau, tel. 05.53.52.83.64.*
***La Roche-Chalais*** *Tourist Bureau, tel. 05.53.90.18.95.*
***Thiviers*** *Tourist Bureau, tel. 05.53.55.12.50.*
***Verteillac*** *Tourist Bureau, tel. 05.53.90.37.78.*

*The GR 436, from Villars to Brantôme, and then the GR 36 enable the walker to discover the wonderful landscapes of the Dronne valley. Open to the public: the enchanting châteaux of Jumilhac-le-Grand, Puyguilhem, Bruzac, Richemont, La Chapelle-Fauchet, Bourdeilles, the abbey of Boschaud, the romanesque churches of Le Ribéracois, the villages of Saint-Jean-de-Côle, Brantôme and Aubeterre.*

## Sites open to visitors in northern Périgord

***Teyjat****, the Town Hall cave*
***La Chaire à Calvin*** *shelter, at* ***Mouthiers-sur-Boëme****:*
*enquire at the Tourist Bureau of* ***Angoulême***
*The* ***Queroy*** *cave, at* ***Chazelle****, tel. 05.45.70.38.14.*
***Angoulême Fine-Arts museum****, tel. 05.45.95.07.69.*

***Nontron*** *Tourist Office, tel. 05.53.56.25.50.*
***Angoulême*** *Tourist Bureau, tel. 05.45.95.16.84.*
***Jumilhac*** *Tourist Bureau, tel. 05.53.52.55.43.*
***Mareuil*** *Tourist Bureau, tel. 05.53.60.99.85.*
***Saint-Pardoux-la-Rivière*** *Tourist Bureau,*
*tel. 05.53.56.79.30.*
***Varaignes*** *Tourist Bureau, tel. 05.53.56.35.76.*
***Javerlhac*** *Tourist Bureau, tel. 05.53.56.30.18.*

*Apart from prehistoric sites, the visitor can also see the châteaux of Jumilhac-le-Grand and Mareuil, the museums of Nontron and Varaignes, the keep of Piégut and the church of Bussière-Badil.*

***Villars cave: the fount hall.***
Photo Pub Image, Périgueux.

## The Dronne valley: Villars, Brantôme and Bourdeilles

Route ⑫

### The Villars cave

The valley of the Dronne, a pretty river dividing the north of the *département* and passing through some of the most beautiful tourist centres of Périgord, holds many important prehistoric sites.

Villars is a village with three marvels; the château of Puyguilhem, the abbey of Boschaud, and a prehistoric splendour. Four kilometres (2.5 miles) to the north-east, the Villars cavern (or Cluzeau cavern), very rich in concretions, is open to the public. Apart from its wonderful concretions, it holds about thirty paintings and engravings, between 15,000 and 17,000 years old. The cave was discovered in 1953, and the wall decorations were found four years later, to everyone's surprise since the region is poor in prehistoric remains. Glory and Breuil worked there first, and then Leroi-Gourhan and G. and B. Delluc. All along the entrance passage there is a line of dots in red ochre and black. Among the most interesting pictures, one can see the famous "blue horse" and, at the end of the cave, as at Lascaux, the drawing of a man being attacked by a bison. On several levels, the cavern forms a network 10 kilometres long (6 miles), one of the biggest in Périgord together with Rouffignac. One finds a real subterranean fairyland during the visit: several hundreds of metres of cave pools, stone masses, eccentrics, cascades, candles, ceilings of stalactites, and draperies. The interest of all this is heightened even further by the wall paintings, certain of which date back more than 17,000 years, even though some are difficult to make out because of the deposits of calcite. There are also clear traces of occupation by the cave bear. There are other caves as well in the Villars ensemble: the Trou, which smokes, the Carrière and several more of lesser importance.

At Saint-Martin-de-Fressengeas, near Thiviers, a decorated cave was discovered in 1990,

***Villars cave: the paintings hall***
Photo Pub Image, Périgueux.

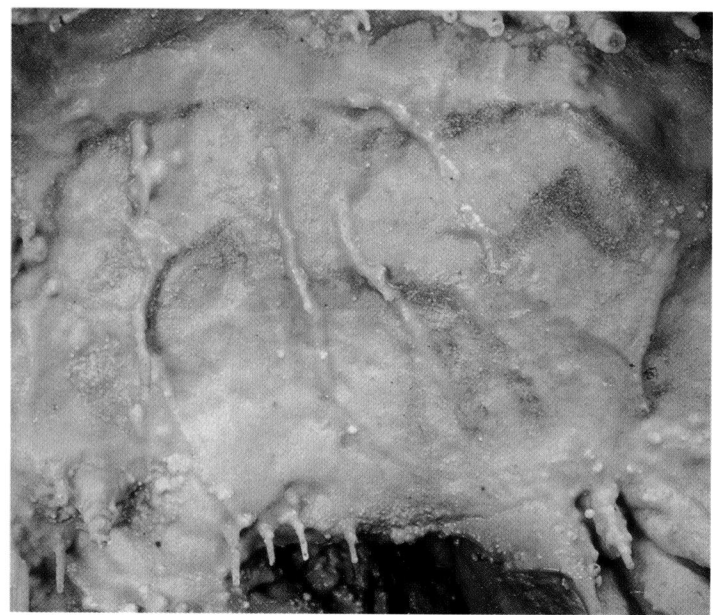

which is exceptionally rich in remains from 1,400 to 900 B.C., still intact. This new "Bronze Age Lascaux" is still being studied.

## Brantôme and the Rebières vale

At the hamlet of Le Fouret, Condat-sur-Trincou possesses a dolmen and a menhir. The latter, in a farmyard, is visible from the road. Five hundred metres away (550 yds), in a wood, like a huge mushroom, there is a fine dolmen, with cupules. One kilometre (half a mile) before Brantôme, visible from the road (D 78) stands the Pierre-Levée dolmen, one of the finest in Périgord, a vast table 5 metres (16 ft.) by 2.5 metres (8 ft.), resting on three stones (one restored), 1.75 metres (6 ft.) to 2.5 metres (8 ft.) high. At Brantôme, the Desmoulin museum displays prehistoric tools from the Rochereil site.

Between Brantôme and Bourdeilles, the Dronne glides peacefully for 10 kilometres (6 miles) between cliffs pitted with grottoes, evidence of one of the greatest concentrations of prehistoric inhabitation apart from the Vézère valley. Two kilometres (about one mile) from Brantôme, the Rebières vale, excavated in 1906 by E. Pittard, is made up of four main shelters, inhabited from the Mousterian to the Magdalenian (100,000 to 10,000 B.C.).

*The Pierre-Levée dolmen, at Brantôme*

On the south slope the Bonhomme shelter presents several Mousterian layers, and then a vast Aurignacian and Perigordian inhabitation. The Festons shelter, which is very similar, has Mousterian remains on its lower terrace, and Aurignacian on its upper terrace. The Durand-Ruel shelter (or Rebière II) provided an abundance of tools from the Aurignacian and Upper Perigordian periods. And then there are the two Recourbie sites which have provided Magdalenian tools.

A little further downstream, Valeuil is an important megalithic centre. Apart from the dolmen of Laprouges, one can see another dolmen, at Beauroulet, at the edge of the D 106, and the Jambe-Grosse menhir, in the Coutoux clearing, near the hamlet of La Besse. Away from the valley, on the right bank, in the commune of Paussac-et-Saint-Vivien three megaliths are concealed. Near Le Breuil, one

***Auroch of the Fourneau du Diable, found near Bourdeilles.* National Museum of Prehistory at Les Eyzies.**

finds the Peyre-Rouyo dolmen and the Peyre-Dermale megalithic ensemble, composed of a big stone monument 6 metres long (20 ft.), with a carved niche and two big irrigated cupules, and also a little menhir. From the D 93, between Paussac and Saint-Vivian, at Prézat-Haut, one can see the big Peyre-Levado dolmen, standing on five supports, one of the finest in Périgord.

## Bourdeilles and the Fourneau du Diable

Bourdeilles also has numerous prehistoric sites. Apart from the aven-cave of Pey de l'Aze (Upper Solutrean), the main site open to visitors is the Fourneau du Diable (Devil's Furnace). Its lower shelf dates from the Gravettian and recent Solutrean. Its upper terrace, with levels from early Solutrean and the end of the Magdalenian, were excavated in 1924 by D. Peyrony, who discovered an engraved block of stone, now in the museum at Les Eyzies, representing eleven aurochs, three of which are very clear, dating from 16,000 B.C. The site has provided remains of portable art and ornaments from various epochs, as well as deposits of colouring materials (crayons of red and yellow ochre and manganese). Higher than Le Fourneau one finds the Bernous cave, engraved with three animal representations (mammoth, bear and rhinoceros), also excavated by D. Peyrony. Abbé Breuil has dated these engravings as Aurignacian. Fonseigner is an open-air prehistoric site, discovered in 1976, with eleven archeological levels from the Mousterian epoch. Finally, the Trou de la Chèvre site (Goat's Hole), where excavations started in 1948, comprises the Chèvre cave, the Francillous shelter and a second shelter. This site was inhabited over a long period. Above the Mousterian, four levels of Châtelperronian were found (35,000 B.C.), making this site a reference site for this epoch. One then finds several Aurignacian levels with traces of hearths, and then the Upper Perigordian.

## Rochereil and the Pont-d'Ambon : at the heart of the Azilian

Downstream from Bourdeilles, between the town and the commune of Grand-Brassac, and not far from the Renamon viewpoint, the Rochereil prehistoric cave was excavated between 1935 and 1939. It has provided portable art dating from the end of the Magdalenian period (10,000 B.C.) and an Azilian sepulchre (8,000 B.C.). The skeleton, although not carbonized itself, was surrounded by a deposit of ashes and burnt earth, evidence of funeral rites. About 2,000 worked stones date from the Magdalenian, together with a remarkable bone industry. The Azilian layer also revealed nearly as many tools. A hundred metres away (110 yds), in the Pont-d'Ambon shelter, excavations carried out since 1970 by G. Célérier have revealed evidence of a transition culture between the final Magdalenian and the Azilian.

## Jovelle-La Tour-Blanche and the megaliths of Ribéracois

Away from the river, to the west of La Tour-Blanche and not far from the ruins of the château of Jovelle, former headquarters of the Black Prince during the Hundred Years' War, the Jovelle prehistoric cave was discovered in 1983. This is decorated with many animal engravings, including a very beautiful head of an ibex and a mammoth with cupules carved out of its side. These works could date back to the very beginning of cave art and could be contemporary with the venerable Pair-Non-Pair cave, in Gironde (30,000 to 25,000 B.C.). In the same area one finds the La Peyzie site (Magdalenian and Azilian), the Brouillard shelter (Mousterian and Aurignacian) and the Sandougne site (Mousterian).

Besides its Palaeolithic sites of Bos du Pic and its Neolithic sites of Mouréloux and Vernode, Tocane, on the left bank, possesses the Vaurélie dolmen and the Margot dolmen, the latter on the Douchapt road between Tocane and Segonzac. Eight kilometres (5 miles) to the south, at Seyssac in Saint-Aquilin, one can see the splendid Pierre-Brune (or Belet) dolmen by the road, raised up on its seven pillars. Excavations revealed arrow tips, a biface and shards of pottery. Saint-Aquilin still guards the great tumulus of Ventadou. After Ribérac, the "lovely river Dronne" passes by Doublaud country, where Festalemps hides a polisher and the fine Bourgeade megalith. At Vanxains, apart from the prehistoric sites of Chancoutier, Brangélie, Javerdhat, Jarretou, Regnac, Jean-Gros and the Camp du Fournet, there is the Sauteranne megalithic alignment and a Bronze Age workshop. A bronze sword, on display at the Périgord museum, was discovered at Saint-Paul-Lizonne.

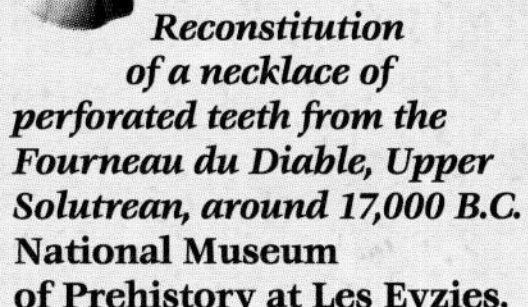

***Reconstitution of a necklace of perforated teeth from the Fourneau du Diable, Upper Solutrean, around 17,000 B.C.***
**National Museum of Prehistory at Les Eyzies.**

### *Azilian, or the end of the Palaeolithic world*

*There was a big climatic change around 10,000 B.C., which made the reindeer move north, and caused the rapid disappearance of a prehistoric civilization which had lasted 25,000 years.*
*In the Azilian era, cave art disappeared completely, and tools were adapted to other game while new funeral rites appeared. In Périgord, the sites of Rochereil and Le Pont-d'Ambon, on the Dronne, and that of Le Peyrat, at Saint-Rabier, are evidence of this short period (10,000 to 8,000 B.C.). The bow and arrow was developed for hunting in the forests. Chipping of tiny flints (or microliths), as tips for arrows, was typical of the following period: the Sauveterrian (8,000 to 6,000 B.C.), present at the Roc du Barbeau and at Sauveterre-la-Lémance.*

## Northern Périgord: from Nontron to Angoulême

Route ⑬

### The Teyjat cave

The Fronsac cave, discovered in 1984, near Vieux Mareuil, contains sexual graffiti dating back to the Magdalenian. To the north-west, in the commune of Champeaux, one finds the prehistoric caves of Puyrignac and, right next to the château of Bernardières, a prehistoric site with the most evocative of names: the Grange des Putes (Whores' Barn)! In March 1986, in the Font-Bargeix cave, whose entrance was dug out as a shelter in the Middle Ages, speleologists have found animal figures dating from the Magdalenian. A Neolithic axe was discovered at Saint-Sulpice-de-Mareuil while La Rochebeaucourt has a Bronze Age workshop.

To the north-east of Nontron, a visitor touring the north of Dordogne in a hurry might not think of stopping at Teyjat. However, he would be wrong, since Teyjat possesses a real treasure several millennia old: a prehistoric decorated cave open to the public. It is in the very centre of the village, between the church and the town hall (whence its name; Town Hall cave). The decorated part has been arranged for the public. The primitive aspect of the rest of the cave gives the visitor the impression that he is back in the heroic times of the first explorers.

After the entry chamber, on the left, on a stalagmitic flow, there are about forty fine engravings divided into six panels. The cave was first excavated in 1880, but it was only between 1903 and 1905 that Peyrony discovered them and they were studied by Abbé Breuil. Horses, deer, reindeer, bison, bears and horned cattle were dated back to the end of the Magdalenian period (about 10,000 B.C.). The ground delivered up tools from the same epoch indicating that this site can be compared with those of neighbouring Angoulême country. The Teyjat point is typical of the Upper Magdalenian. The very accomplished and realistic style of the engravings (the frieze of cattle in the last panel is famous, and for good reason) marks the peak of the art of cave decoration in the Palaeolithic era. At the end of the cave, a well gives access to a lower floor and an underground river. The Mège shelter, fifty metres (55 yds) from the cave, was inhabited in the Magdalenian. Although it cannot pretend to rival Font-de-Gaume or les Combarelles, Teyjat is worth a visit for Prehistory enthusiasts. Incidentally, better signposting would attract the public it deserves. One can still see the remains of a dolmen at Veaubrunet: the Pierre-Plate (Flat-Stone) dolmen.

And then again, there is the Fixard menhir, at Piégut, and, next to the D 77, at Saint-Jory-de-Chalais, La Roulandie, the big La Jolinie dolmen, 4 metres long (13 ft.). The cupules carved into it are said to be the tracks of Herod's horse following the Holy Family, hidden under the dolmen. At Jumilhac-le-Grand, the tumulus of La Lande de Prunou contains funerary remains from the Iron Age.

### A step into Charente

Prehistory does not end at the gates of Périgord. Entering Charente, the Bandiat and Tardoire rivers overflow with prehistoric sites of great importance. The Montgaudier cave, at Montbron, and the Placard cave at Vilhonneur, contain engravings dating from the end of the Magdalenian (11,000 B.C.). The La Chaise caves and shelters, at Vouthon, and the Fontéchevade cave at Orgedeuille, guard Mousterian remains, and even Tayacian for the latter (200,000 B.C.). The Rancogne sepulchral cave dates from the end of the Bronze Age (2,500 B.C.). In Chazelle, the Queroy cave, open to the public, has remains from the Artenician (end of the Neolithic, 4,000 B.C.) up to the Tène civilization (Iron Age, 500 B.C.). The Artenician takes its name from the Artenac sepulchral cave at Saint-Mary, a little to the north. Not far away, at La Rochette, the Duffaits sepulchral cave dates from the Bronze Age.

Further south, at Sers, the Roc vale, inhabited in the Aurignacian period and the Perigordian, has revealed a Solutrean sepulchre. It holds the Roc de Sers shelter where, in 1927, about twenty engraved stones were found dating from 17,000 years ago. South of Angoulême, at Mouthiers-sur-Boëme, the sculpted shelter of La Chaire à Calvin, open to visitors, displays a frieze of horses dating from the early Magdalenian (15,000 B.C.). Not far away, the Grotte des Rois and the Vachons shelter were inhabited in the Aurignacian period. Right next to the Périgord border, in the Gardes commune, the La Quina prehistoric site, excavated as early as 1906, and which held the remains of 27 Neanderthals, gave its name to one of the Mousterian cultures. Leaving the north of Périgord, less than 20 kilometres (12 miles) away, in Charente, one thus finds a complete summary of Prehistory.

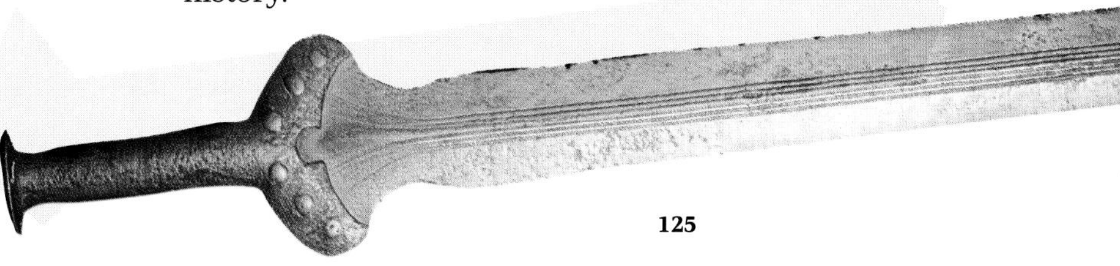

***Gaulish sword in bronze: the end of Prehistory.***
**Périgord Museum, Périgueux.**

## Index of Prehistoric Sites referred to in the text

(**in bold** : sites open to the public)

## Museums with prehistoric collections



We would like to present our sincere thanks to the owners
of the sites who lent us photographs to illustrate this book.

## Contents



**Graphic design: Terre de Brume**


ISBN 2 7373 2260.X - Dépôt légal : mai 1997 - N° d'éditeur : 3648.02.1,5.01.99
Imprimé par Mame imprimeurs à Tours (37)